CW00749939

Beware Wet Paint *Designs by Alan Fletcher*

Beware Wet Paint *Designs by Alan Fletcher*   Commentary by Jeremy Myerson

Marcel Duchamp used the phrase 'Beware Wet Paint'
to remind us that it takes time to judge the worth
of work. This book looks at thirty-five years of
Alan Fletcher's work; some of the most recent may
not yet be dry.

This is also a book about the design process, the
thinking behind the solutions and the methods used to
resolve them. To show this more clearly the examples
illustrated are, in the main, not displayed in their
original context but as images in their own right.

Each example is accompanied by a full commentary
by Jeremy Myerson. Four essays give further critical
and biographical insight to the work, and the man.

Contents

The idea that something as banal and so benign as dribbles of paint could offer a surprise or present a threat is curiously appropriate to Alan Fletcher's work. His seemingly innocent, innocuous, often naive images appear familiar, but there is usually a sting in the tail which makes you look twice. Aspects of his work may seem the same, but they're different in some way. Perhaps the reason for this is that one of the most immediate and striking features of his vast portfolio is how familiar images and icons recur in an ever-broadening range of contexts.

He is unafraid to revisit the same idea, thought or technique, obsessively reworking it to achieve a better execution or stronger effect, to give it an extra twist to deepen the meaning, or to extend its potential, or just to amuse (himself as much as anyone else). He recognizes this trait in his work and has no hang-ups about it: 'Monet painted the façade of Rouen cathedral at least thirty times,' he points out, 'and who knows how many times Hokusai drew Mount Fuji?'

What are those favourite things which so command his interest? Human features, mazes, stars, and letterforms repeat themselves, often in unexpected guises. A labyrinth originally designed for a mural in Warren Street, the London Underground station, reappears in different configurations and situations such as a maze on a congratulations card, or in three dimensions as a toy. A star can be put to use as the basis for the corporate identity of an Arab bank, only to crop up again in more vibrant fashion in a calendar to express fireworks. Sometimes objects and things will be used in tandem on the same project, such as in the poster for a student seminar which combines two old cardboard 35mm transparency holders with typewriter-generated blocks of type to create a face.

That these images recur is less important than the manner and context in which they are deployed. And the problem here, he says, is how to transfer a thought from one head to another without it becoming garbled in the process.

For one so associated with free-flowing creativity, Fletcher admits that for many years he felt inhibited about directly expressing his ideas through drawing. A throwback to the days when he was a student at the Central School in the 1950s. 'Those who were less skilled in drawing tended to take refuge in typography, persuading themselves it was a more worthy activity than illustration,' he remembers. 'There was also a reaction against the "personality" poster artists of previous generations and admiration for the "Swiss school", which had engendered the concept of the graphic designer as anonymous engineer.' Strongly influenced as a student by the Bauhaus, it was only later on that he found a rich creative source of expression in his own individual, quirky style – a style expressed through simple materials, primitive techniques, commonplace objects, and anything else which happened to be to hand. And a dedication to finding a simple direct solution to stretch the boundaries of image-making.

Many projects – the incorporation of the alphabet into a pair of gates for his own home, the posters for IBM, or the cover for *The Art Book* – reflect a fascination with letters. He is keen to make a distinction between letters and typefaces. He feels letters are not governed by rules. Whereas typefaces are a reflection of the graphic designer's intervention in the alphabet to set regulations governing proportion, appearance, and so on. Even computer-generated typography, although liberating itself from one set of conventions, has established another.

His argument is that those typographic purists who are offended by his liberated approach – turning letters into icons in their own right – are simply confusing letters with typefaces. As he has been taught by some of the world's greatest typographers – from Anthony Froshaug to Bradbury Thompson – it is reasonable to conclude that he knows what he's talking about.

One of Fletcher's most famous preoccupations are his Feedback guidebooks, which are a collection of recommendations of where to stay, where to eat or what to visit, in cities around the world. These are compiled from despatches sent in by his international network of friends – most of them fellow designers, architects, and photographers. Feedback provides a remarkable grapevine of information, reflecting the tastes and interests of the creative community. However, its instigator, a much-travelled man, is also a master at expressing the graphic notion of place. This is no easy task. Perhaps the hardest job for any designer concerns the communication of abstract concepts. How does one sum up a country in a single image? How, for that matter, does one graphically express searing heat or piercing cold? And even

yet more difficult – how can one communicate an atmosphere of hospitality, or the despair of poverty?

Fletcher's methods in crystallizing these expressions often depend on an economy of means, the result of his own imposition of constraints to define the limitations. It is almost as though he cannot function unless he works within tight parameters; whether it is by restricting himself to just pen, pencil and paper to suggest the seasons, or by confining himself to a collection of old printed ephemera to construct the Chinese horoscope. He seems to be in some way affronted by total freedom and only by forcing himself into a tight corner can he find the essence he is trying to communicate.

In developing such a rigorous approach he shows extraordinary self-discipline, not to say masochism. Often he will subject himself to painstaking work just to get the image right in his own mind. He will decide to draw a seascape in lines, and then carefully make sure that they do not touch one another – as in his image of the view of America by Columbus for a poster to commemorate the 500th anniversary of its discovery in 1492. Or restrict himself in creating a recognizable array of cats using only the wrong end of a wood dip pen.

Many of the designs reflect an extensive knowledge of art and design history. They often unashamedly borrow from these sources, whether the flag scenes prompted by a Raoul Dufy painting for a depiction of a French fête, the tiny figures in a crowded beach scene which he candidly admits were influenced by Henri Michaux, or a play on Mondrian's *Boogie Woogie* painting of Manhattan in interpreting a view of Amsterdam.

Much of his work – especially those more personal graphic observations – shows 'a condensation of sensations'. Difficult and intangible subjects such as seasonal weather or poverty are reduced to simple icons which instantly invoke their message: a clothes peg accompanied by a child's writing becomes a forlorn figure, a typographic design drenched in vivid fluorescent inks creates a green field with red flowers to represent July (the year was 1968, a reminder that he has been mastering abstract expressions for many years).

He has been engaged in graphic games for a long time. For a designer who thinks deeply about his subject and perseveres to develop solutions to problems, it may be inappropriate to describe him as a player of games, but there is an irresistible sense of fun in his work. He is the 'game' boy whose designs are suffused with the personal ritual of play. Some are short and simple: the addition of a few lines to transform one thing into another, as in a memorable 'Designers' Saturday' poster; the subtraction of elements to produce solutions of the greatest economy, as in his now classic logo for the Victoria & Albert Museum; or the drawing of a cup of Greek coffee, with Greek coffee. Even the complicated games tempt you to join in – as in a connect-the-dots design for April in a 1972 calendar (1,972 dots, naturally) – until half way through it is realized that it begins on April Fool's Day and that the joke is on you.

Fletcher plays with interchanging positive and negative shapes, manipulates light and shade; deliberately distorts dimensions and perspectives, visually exploits the nuances inherent in ideograms, tangrams and palindromes. Some of the visual conceits are as much a balancing act as his design for a wedding invitation which precariously arranges the letters of Amore on top of one another. He enjoys standing ideas on their head.

He also delights in the art of the ambiguous, leaving the viewer unsure of what the image really represents. Is a vase of flowers for an advertising agency emblem within the picture frame itself or on the table in front of the picture ? Is that Z logo for the Zinc Development Association really three-dimensional ? Even when he has set up a positive image in the viewer's mind, he does occasionally undermine it – as with a splatter of black ink to deface the colourful letters of Napoli.

However, the casual presentation of some of the games disguises the graft that has gone into making them work. A prize-winning poster for Daimler Benz to commemorate the 100th anniversary of the automobile looks simple until one appreciates the mental leap involved in making an automobile out of three numerals.

Sometimes his enthusiasms require the co-operation of his designer friends. Over the years he has amassed a unique collection of table napkins as a result of asking his dinner companions to draw on one as a memento of the evening. Not surprisingly

many of the results are equally personal, idiosyncratic and unpredictable.

But to suggest that his career has been all play and no work would be wrong. He has had creative freedoms in his time – often designing for cultural and charitable causes – able to make his own mark without the onerous presence of a grey corporate committee to smother the idea. But not all projects or briefs allow the game boy to operate. And not all clients are adventurous or sophisticated enough to accept (or appreciate) an offbeat solution.

Indeed, one of the most interesting aspects of the portfolio is that he has spent a large part of his time and energy on projects which by their definition do not come creatively uncompromised; some of his best-known designs have been developed under the toughest commercial and operational conditions. Corporate identities for multinational giants, sign systems for public spaces.

Difficult challenges have included the original identity for the Design Council (guaranteed to draw the flak of the entire UK profession), a sign system for the interior of the Lloyd's Building by Richard Rogers, a promotional figure for Pirelli to rival the Michelin Man, and a symbol and housestyle for a World Expo in Vienna and Budapest. These are but a few of his projects which required patience, tact, stamina as well as skill.

By his own admission, some of these assignments have been less than successful. A sign system for the cavernous and confusing spaces of the Victoria & Albert Museum in London, has not been allowed to work as conceived because inadequate budgets have meant piecemeal or partial implementation. His large three-dimensional graphic sculptures for Stansted Airport terminal met with the irresistible combined opposition of the British Airports Authority, HM Customs, Passport Control et al.

There have been some singular successes too. The acceptance by the client of his proposals for a piece of punched tape as the basis for the famous Reuters logotype, or the identity and housestyle for the Commercial Bank of Kuwait, or a light-hearted symbol for the Munich Oktoberfest, must make all the surrounding heartache of international design – the rejected concepts, the missed planes, the intransigent clients, the lonely hotels – worthwhile.

Whatever the scale of the task, Fletcher never loses sight of his own artistic responsibilities or grasp of his own creative agenda. The financial charts in an annual report, for example, become an exercise in colour theory. Even outside the graphic discipline, the controversial issue of what to do with the fire-damaged wing in Windsor Castle – to restore or to redesign? – receives a typically robust and iconoclastic response. Fletcher argues that the answer is to 'leave the gutted and charred remains exactly as they are', cover them with a glass canopy and project slide and video images into the space to show the various decorative styles of the past – Gothic, Baroque, Victorian – plus the conflagration itself. It is innovative thinking of this kind which has enabled him to prove as imaginative in meeting unorthodox challenges as when he just has himself to please.

Underlying the traits which characterize his work, there is one governing theme: the search for the concept. For all of the games, the wit, the revisiting of favourite subjects, the offbeat and often quirky approaches, the unearthing of ideas lies at the heart of his craft. 'That to me is what design is all about. The rest is just layout.' And he goes on to explain, 'I'm quite broad about ideas. Putting certain colours together could be an idea, or it could be a literary idea, or an optical idea. Every job has to have an idea. Otherwise it would be like writing a book without really saying anything.'

Some ideas may result purely from his penchant for discovery, where he surrenders himself to the investigation, following where it leads. These are happy accidents, as seen in the poster for the National Portrait Gallery in London – a caricature of a royal person achieved through the cutting and reassembling of other people's portraits. Or in the symbol to promote the 50th anniversary of the National Gallery of Art in Washington DC derived from counting the stars on the American flag.

Others ideas frame the solution in a more logical way, as in a symbol for an organization promoting unity between Islamic countries which was created from interlocking crescents visible in the pattern of the silk cord of an Arabic headdress. Or they result from the simplest of observations: a letterhead for a film production company resulted directly from noting how the clients' white shirts merged into the table during a late-night meeting.

Fletcher is also confident enough to borrow from the past: a famous 1930s advertisement by Cassandre becomes the basis for a poster for D&AD (properly credited, of course); he is also uninhibited enough to borrow from himself – a hand-drawn vision of land seen from across the sea, which first appeared as a representation of Denmark in a calendar, is repeated on a larger scale as the poster for Columbus's first sighting of the Americas.

Ideas can spring out of the method and technology. His own handwriting (as in the representation of Stonehenge), or by the computer (the gypsy figure on the Gitanes cigarette pack being turned into its shadow). It doesn't matter where ideas come from or what methods are used to make them work – he is only interested in making sure he digs them up. And in a long career, he observes that he finds the process never seems to get any easier.

Beware Wet Paint is divided into sections which present different facets of Alan Fletcher's thinking, personality and approach. It is not an exhaustive catalogue of his entire portfolio of work, nor is it a comprehensive analysis of his complete career. Rather, it presents snapshots of the insights of a creative mind at work through the medium of more than 200 designs, grouped in ways which aid understanding of the tangential nature of the interrelationship of ideas – and accompanied by some of his views on the design process.

Over thirty-five years, he has produced so many memorable designs that one could argue that an entirely different group of projects could have been chosen to suit the purposes of this publication. Fletcher means 'maker of arrows', and I believe this selection is representative of a designer whose ability to hit the target again and again with such clarity and purpose has now become legendary. This book explains how he aims his sights, loads his arrow, pulls back the bow – and lets fly. Also, how he occasionally shoots himself in the foot.

EVAPORATE
THEY
REALITY
INTO
MASSAGED
ARE
IDEAS
UNLESS

AF

Where do ideas come from ? The question is difficult to answer. Practice and experience can place the designer in the right frame of mind to generate ideas, but at some point intuition takes over. Ideas emerge in all kinds of different ways, often by chance.

Sometimes it happens when the barriers of common sense are down at the end of a long hard day, whilst daydreaming or when a happy accident suggests the solution. The trigger could be word association, or a deliberate attempt to pay homage to a classic design, or an unlikely combination of diverse thoughts. Whatever the route, every job has to have an idea as a starting point. Here are some ideas.

Ideas can generate their own ideas. This instantly recognizable montage, for instance, arrived by luck. The brief was for a poster (left) to mark the opening of the new twentieth-century wing at the National Portrait Gallery in London. After exploring different routes, Fletcher decided to construct a generic portrait from photographs supplied by the Gallery.

Portraits of Famous British Personalities
from 1945 to the 1990's are on permanent
exhibition at the 20th Century Galleries
in the National Portrait Gallery.
Free admission. Open 10 to 5pm weekdays,
10 to 6pm Saturdays and 2 to 6pm Sundays.
Nearest ⊕ Leicester Square & Charing Cross

He randomly cut out eyes, mouths and noses and began arranging the pieces into a face. Parts of Sir Laurence Olivier, Ceri Richards, Julian Trevelyan, Sir John Pope-Hennessy, Frank Leavis and Graham Sutherland make up the composite portrait. It was when he put down the ear that he saw the likeness.

Unsure whether he had achieved a recognizable representation of the heir to the throne or not, he decided to test it on six people in Pentagram's studio. The first five immediately said that it was Charles. The sixth (an American), hesitatingly, proffered Buster Keaton. With a score like that, he felt he'd got it right.

Ceri Richards

Sir Laurence Olivier

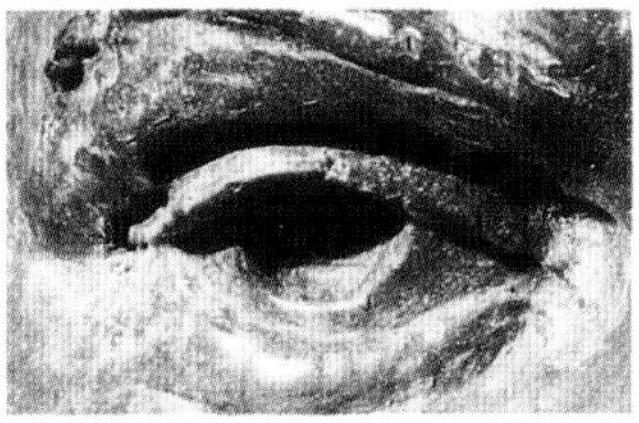

Graham Sutherland

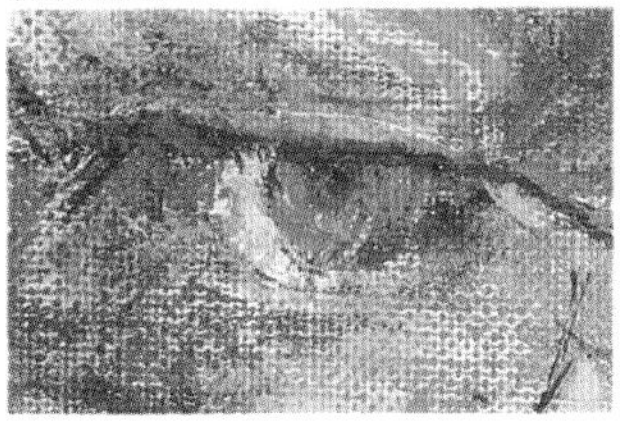

Frank Leavis

Julian Trevelyan

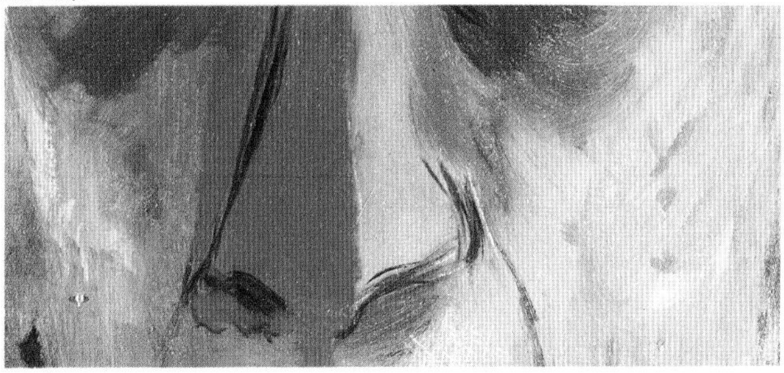

Sir John Pope-Hennessy

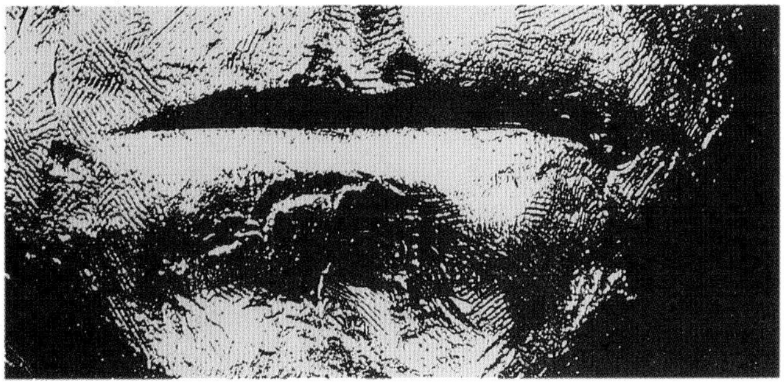

Some ideas emerge out of a particular situation or
circumstance. When three film commercials directors
wanted an identity for their new company, Fletcher
visited them one evening in their large, dimly lit studios.
As the discussions developed, and the wine flowed, he
noticed that their white shirts merged into the whiter
conference table. That impression became the basis for
their photographic letterhead (opposite) and housestyle.
Sometimes, ideas generated this casually don't survive
scrutiny in the cold light of day. This one did.

Asked by the Polish government to design a poster commemorating the 50th anniversary of the invasion by Hitler, Fletcher spent days floundering around without getting anywhere – until he wrote down the two dates. The answer had been under his nose all the time. A brilliant solution, even if it doesn't work in America where they write the month first, then the day and the year.

The idea for these ashtrays came when travelling on top of a bus down Westbourne Grove to the studio. An unsolicited mental image arrived, complete in all its details: a shape resembling Dutch Edam cheese with two identical halves made from a single mould, providing both base and lid, or two separate ashtrays with serrated teeth to hold the halves together or grip the cigarette. First manufactured in Italy they were instantly copied by other manufacturers and yet he never received a penny from anyone. When he decided to take legal action, one of the producers became so incensed he smashed the moulds with a sledgehammer.

The genuine version has a credit stamped on the inner edge, the others don't. As he recounts: 'I saw half of one (with broken teeth) on a bank counter in Buenos Aires holding paper clips, another on the dais of a Bangkok bar where girls blow smoke rings from personal places, and on a designer's desk who told me he salvaged it from a rabbit hutch in Norfolk.' Easy come, easy go.

1.9.39

1 September 1939: marks the outbreak
of the second world war when Nazi
Germany invaded Poland. This year
we commemorate those who lost their
lives and families: 1 September 1989.

1.9.89

AIGA WASHINGTON PRESENTS **AN EVENING WITH PENTAGRAM** ALAN FLETCHER, KIT HINRICHS, WOODY PIRTLE. 27 FEBRUARY 1990. LECTURE 7.30PM. DUPONT PLAZA HOTEL, EMBASSY HALL BALLROOM, 1500 NEW HAMPSHIRE AVENUE, NW WASHINGTON, DC 20036.

PROJECT**2001**

Word association

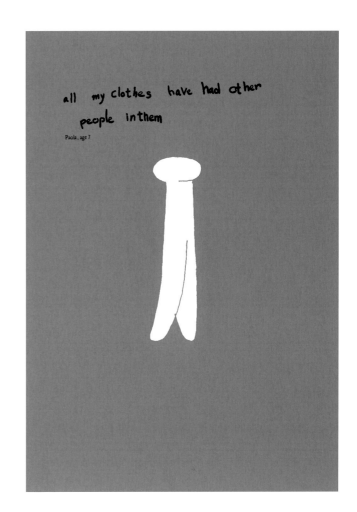

all my clothes have had other people in them

Paola, age 7

There is a game in which one thing leads to another through word association. For example: sausage – pig – bristle – brush. Sometimes the thought for a graphic arrives in a similar fashion. The poster on the right is one of a series designed for IBM which is aimed at stirring the conscience of the employees to contribute to charities selected by the corporation. In this case the sequence of thoughts was: poverty – second-hand clothes – laundry day – washing line – clothes peg – human figure.

The solution for a poster (opposite) announcing an Evening with Pentagram, a lecture programme organized by the American Institute of Graphic Arts in Washington DC, was arrived at via the same route. As there were fourteen Pentagram partners at the time, Fletcher decided to develop the theme of an evening sky studded with stars. Stars led to pentagrams – all fourteen of them drawn as cavorting five-pointed zoomorphic figures. Yet when the poster was printed, only thirteen stars appeared. It transpired that one had fallen off the artwork while in transit. Some of the partners asked Fletcher who he'd left off. Making the best of an embarrassing situation, he just shrugged his shoulders and gave a knowing smile.

Project 2001, an initiative of the Royal Society of Arts, seeks to celebrate the millennium with an investment in the 'social capital' of the United Kingdom through two thousand and one projects. The emblem of a petalled flower has less defined associations of fruition and fortune. However, the thought behind the single petal was derived from the children's games of 'tinker, tailor, soldier, sailor...' or more appropriately, 'this year, next year, sometime, never', or the selection of one from many.

Max Ponty – the celebrated French designer of the Gitanes cigarette pack – shares with Marcel Jacno (of Gauloise fame) the distinction of being probably the only designer ever credited on a cigarette pack. Since the imposition of advertising curbs on smoking, Gitanes has sought to promote their brand by annual exhibitions on interpretations of the Ponty gypsy. First, famous painters were invited to participate, then top photographers and then well-known graphic designers.

The brief specified that the gypsy had to be the major element on the poster. On close inspection Fletcher decided that he didn't like the silhouette, and so he tried a variety of ways to disguise the figure. At first he thought the answer lay in doing a vague freehand descriptive drawing, the pictorial sketch (below) being an early attempt. However in the end the problem became the solution. By turning the gypsy upside-down and manipulating it on a computer – his first-ever project using this technology – he converted the figure into shadow and, at the same time, implied a third dimension. 'You often have to read between the lines when you get a brief.' His entry was singled out to promote the exhibition.

a homage to Max Ponty

EAMS

Design is what happens between conceiving an idea and fashioning the means to carry it out.

Whether it's big stuff like painting a picture, writing a book, conducting a military campaign,

creating a commercial enterprise, or small stuff like organizing a party. In short, design

is an intelligent equation between purpose and construction. A few people also earn their

living by giving form to the amenities of life in manufacture, communication and place.

They call themselves designers. They are the blue collar workers of the art world.   AF

This section demonstrates how colours can play a conscious role in creative problem-solving, how they have an ability to convey emotion, alter perceptions, and trigger associations. However, the meaning of colours varies from culture to culture. In England, for example, you are green with envy, whereas in Japan envy turns you purple (see pages 42 and 43).

Colour is used in a number of ways. He treats it with subtlety or with brute force. It might be haphazardly applied, or matched with painstaking precision, but it is rarely used for decorative or arbitrary reasons.

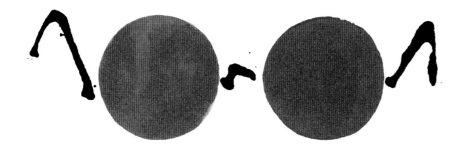

Take a rainbow. This one doesn't show the whole thing and it doesn't even depict the right colours. But that doesn't matter. It's a notation of a rainbow and says enough to convey the impression without descending into cliché. This kind of economy and clarity of purpose extends right through Fletcher's work, encompassing a spectrum which ranges from subtle to super-bold.

The idea which lay behind a blinding fluorescent ink colour contrast calendar for Olivetti was to forcibly alter the ambience of the office in which it was hung each month. The Italian printer needed sunglasses to print the job, and the fluorescent ink supplier who helped on the specifications thought it was extremely vulgar. The typographic page for the month of June creates a vibrant scene of red flowers in a green field.

At the other end of the scale is a more delicate exercise. When a Kuwait consortium commissioned an annual report, Fletcher decided to turn the financial diagrams into demonstrations of a colour theory. In the example shown (page 33) the two vertical turquoise bars are exactly the same colour and only appear different due to an interaction with the colour backgrounds. This is known as the Bezold Effect.

Colour used in a less controlled way can be seen in the lurid sunset representing Italy (as Naples) in a calendar on the European Community. Here, he dampened the paper and liberally tipped watercolours over it, closed his eyes, and quickly tilted the paper back and forth.

Compare this with the studied treatment for a field of tiny vivid blue flowers in which each single flower is a different shade of blue from cerulean to indigo. The presence of the one yellow flower was to make the blues appear bluer.

Every year an opera season is held in the magnificent landscaped grounds of an early plantation house in Barbados. The elements for the house, garden and pool, are assembled from tropical hues, to produce an evocative and colourful symbol for a Caribbean festival. The intense yellow glow of the pumpkin for Halloween sets the occasion by using a different kind of contrast.

The plate of black olives is just that – a subtle use of different black inks to challenge the theory that black isn't a colour. The deliberate combination of pink, as a background, with a yellow Easter chick creates a sensation which is both cute and sentimental, an effect other graphic devices might struggle to match.

Colour can also be applied to prod the sub-conscious. For a number of different Polaroid posters, promoting a new colour film, Fletcher created an intriguing Rorschach test. This is a diagnostic technique used by psychologists to get patients to say what they think an abstract form represents. The design was made by dropping colours onto a flat sheet of paper, which he then folded in half, and squashed. Opened up, it revealed a picture rich in potential meaning.

L	0	2	9	16	23	30
M	0	3	10	17	24	G
M	0	4	11	18	25	I
G	0	5	12	19	26	U
V	0	6	13	20	27	G
S	0	7	14	21	28	N
D	1	8	15	22	29	O

Financial diagram

Hysterical sunset

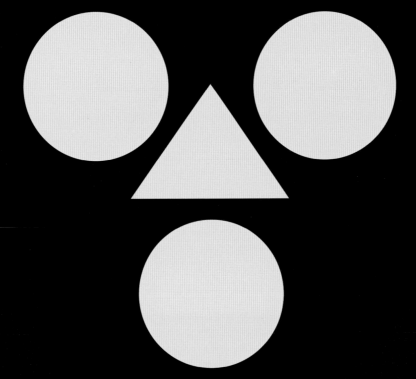

A commercial Rorschach test

ENVY

PASSION

EMBARRASSMENT

TEMPER

FEAR

COWARDICE

DEPRESSION

MOOD

Trying to explain how to ride a bicycle is notoriously difficult. The same distance lies between experience and theory in describing the design process. To my mind defining design as problem solving smacks more of routine work than creative thinking. The fact is designers enjoy playing with problems.

They treat them as a personal challenge and so if someone else asks how they came up with an idea you'll probably hear what the designer thinks you expect to hear. Anything from it just popped up in the head, the result of a mystical experience like a Llama levitating by reversing his polarities or something magical like making a leopard change its spots.

For myself I try to sum up the situation, back in edgeways, and cast around for ideas on which to hang further ideas. It's an intuitive process involving search, discovery, recognition and evaluation. Rejection or development. There are no specific rules or recipes. One might slip through a sequence of actions in seconds, sweat through step by step, start backwards, move randomly from one point to another, or do what surfers call 'hang ten' – get your toes into the board and ride the crest of the wave.

However, there are three essential conditions. The first is the capability for cerebral acrobatics so the mind can juggle the elements while freewheeling around the possibilities. The second is a mind set with the credulity of a child, the dedication of an evangelist, the spadework of a navvy. And the third is sufficient motivation to kiss a lot of frogs before finding a prince. All of which adds up to just one thing. An aim to reach that condensation of sensations which – Matisse said – 'constitutes a picture'.

AF

4. Pidgin graphics

A characteristic of the work is that it often sidesteps
conventional techniques to use a graphic shorthand.
For instance the few scribbles shown here conjure
up the image of a strutting cockerel. A few scissored
shapes can convey the blinding flash of an exploding
firework. A splatter of black ink can express pollution.

In the same way that pidgin English bridges the gap
between different languages by conjuring up mental
images (pidgin for a carpenter's saw is a 'pull him he
come, push 'im he go'), so do the graphics reviewed
in this section.

He frequently makes images with the barest of means. Take this preliminary rough in which by cutting three pieces out of a square and carefully postitioning them four legs, a tail and horns are formed. A snip off the corner makes the head. An animal is born out of an uncompromising geometric shape.

This technique was used to simulate an impression of fireworks, a page from a calendar to celebrate Guy Fawkes Night. The explosion was created by taking five squares of paper – black, white, red, blue and yellow – and by scissoring a star out of each square, thus creating ten stars. Overlapping and interlocking the positive and negative pieces produced a starburst. The random speckle of ink splats implied flicker – a design which deliberately sets out to make the viewer blink. The result is an optical sensation achieved with maximum effect from minimum means. Fletcher admits a certain guilt in using coloured paper, pointing out that Matisse painted the paper he used for his cut-outs.

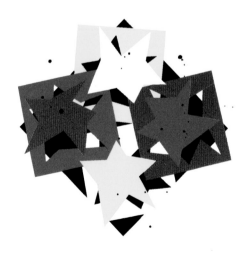

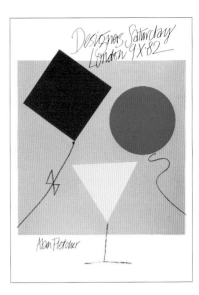

One of his graphic devices is adroitly to add lines to transform a shape from one thing into something else. A commission to design a poster for the annual Designers Saturday, an open day held by design-conscious furniture showrooms in London, came with a completely open brief. Fletcher characteristically set about imposing his own tight constraints. He decided to try out Kandinsky's theory, which relates specific colours to specific forms, and selected the three most basic shapes and the three most obvious colours and then put them on an anonymous grey background. The addition of pencilled lines converted the elements into a lively party scene.

The same game is played for the London Transport poster (opposite), which aimed to encourage people to take a bus when they go shopping. Here a prosaic bar code is made into a stylish carrier bag. A creative addition to the sum of the parts.

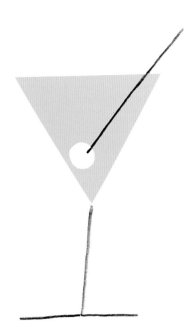

An economical rearrangement can also be an innovative move. This can be seen in the poster opposite, an invitation to an anniversary event held by an advertising agency. Two circles, one in yellow and one in white, were each cut in half and carefully superimposed to produce two champagne glasses. The juxtaposition of the glasses suggests the 'clink', and the blue-black background tells us the party was held in the evening.

A picture on a postcard for a friend in Provence took shape by subtracting a circle from a triangle to create both an onion in the vermouth (a Gibson) and the sun in the sky. The addition of lines generates the stem of a glass, cocktail stick and sunshine.

Geers Gross invites you to celebrate their 25th anniversary on Friday 16 June from 6 pm onwards. Eating, drinking, dancing, music (and maybe a little fooling around) on the roof terrace of their offices at 110 St Martin's Lane, London WC2.

A STATEMENT AGAINST POLLUTION. A poster commissioned by NAPOLI '99 Foundation as a contribution towards the cultural image of the city.

Splattering

A familiar ploy is to set an idea up in the viewer's mind and then to make a sudden intervention which totally undermines and transforms the message. Take this design on a poster for a cultural foundation in Naples which promotes support for the restoration of the city's heritage. The subject, 'A Statement Against Pollution', was emphasized by defacing it with black blotches. The P and O of Napoli were overlapped to make the name (and target) larger, but the task of graphic pollution was less simple than it seems. To achieve the desired effect he dropped the ink from a balcony and although he made a terrible mess on the floor, persisted until he had what he wanted. This radical solution reflects a preoccupation with contrast: the formal letters and informal splats, black and *tutti frutti* colours; the themes of renovation and desecration.

Splatters can also imply flowers, as seen in the postcard (right), one of a colourful set produced for a Japanese corporation. The visual similarity between blots and blooms is reinforced by his caption. Ink blots can also emulate musical notes, and when combined with a stave-like word they neatly illustrate the concept at the heart of the axiom by Walter Pater which featured on a poster for IBM

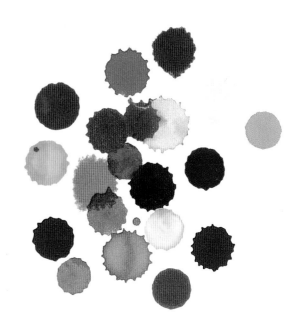

A bouquet of colours

"All art constantly aspires towards the condition of music." Walter Pater

Tearing can be construed as destructive. But in the right hands it can also be constructive. In a calendar on the signs of the Zodiac the depiction of two profiles for Gemini, the twins, was made by tearing a face in half. The thought behind the poster (opposite) is established by tearing off a corner of a rectangle.

At an exhibition of the designer, Willem Sandberg, Fletcher noticed that Sandberg, another devotee of torn paper, first perforated outlines in paper with a pin before he tore the paper. Such attention to detail must obviously impress him, as he self-critically observes that sometimes his own tearing is too casual. His state of mind is one of constant evaluation and re-evaluation.

No man is an island,
entire of itself;
every man is a piece
of the continent,
a part of the main.

John Donne

Another aspect of his work is using whatever is to hand. A designer who once worked with him asked if he'd design her a special birthday card. Looking through his collection of printed ephemera he managed to locate the relevant numbers. As you can see from the collage, she was 24 on the 30th July in 1986. The composition was driven by the sequence of the dates, and the actual sizes of the scraps of paper which carried them.

The image of the cat (opposite) was prompted by an observation made by Georg Lichtenberg, the German scientist and philosopher. The cat was constructed by folding a sheet of old typewriter carbon paper – an exceedingly difficult task as the carbon comes off and the thin paper has a wilful static of its own. The reverse side happened to be printed in a linear pattern. By carefully manoeuvring the folds, he cut two slots so that when they were folded back they became eyes with lashes.

Much of Fletcher's work is done for his own pleasure. Sometimes it may reappear in a commercial context. Sometimes a commercial design might be recycled and redefined. Work and leisure is a seamless activity.

Overleaf

This scene for a poster, entitled a 'Night on the Tiles', was represented by cats freely drawn in ink with the wrong end of a wooden dip pen. It was a hit or miss exercise. The essence of 'catness' is implied by typical postures, not by details. He relies a lot on chance and thinks of it 'as the art of taking risks'.

'It's astonishing
that cats always have
two holes cut in their coats
in exactly the same place
as their eyes'.

Georg Christoph Lichtenberg
(1742-1799)

Rick Poynor **in conversation** with Alan Fletcher

What made you decide to leave Pentagram after 20 years? A combination of factors. I had some terrific jobs, but one after the other, almost at the same time, they died, mainly because the clients were having a hard time economically. They just canned the work, which I found disappointing and frustrating. I was taking jobs that I wouldn't normally have wanted to take because I needed the work in order to help feed the crew. It wasn't something I enjoyed doing. I suppose it had probably happened two or three times before. Three times is enough! Another reason is that I really enjoy doing more personal work, as opposed to having to deal with large, complicated programmes for clients. It was difficult for me to do the sort of thing I wanted for that kind of project. I pulled it off a few times, but it's not so easy. Anyway, I decided that I'd be in a better position to pick and choose on my own.

Was this something you had always expected to do one day? Not particularly. I'm not a planner, not even for next week let alone for next year. I never really thought about it. Pentagram started with very few people and has ended up with a lot of people and bosses. I wasn't staying in exactly the same situation, but one undergoing constant change. Eventually I wanted a bigger change and I thought, if I don't do it now it's probably going to be too late.

What kind of work did you want to do? Well, it was more a case of avoiding the kind of work that I didn't want to do. Complex projects which require interminable meetings and administration, a lot of stroking and people management. Certainly I prefer projects where I find the content or subject interesting. For instance I work with Phaidon who publish fine-art books. That's more stimulating than dog food. Also for Domus magazine which is mainly concerned with contemporary architecture, design and cultural issues. I don't have a moral stance about which jobs I do, it's just that I'd sooner be involved with intelligent people on stimulating projects.

Was that scary after the continuous flow of design projects at Pentagram? I didn't leave with any work and had nothing for the first two or three months. After the first few weeks, I thought, 'I could have made a big mistake here', as I have to earn a living because I've never actually saved anything. Do I get scared about that kind of thing? Not really, probably because I'm a survivor.

You've done a lot of work over the years that is immediately recognizable as your own. How do you go about getting what you want from a client? Smile! I operate best with a certain kind of client. There has to be a rapport. It's not like dealing with your greengrocer, which is a strict buying and selling interaction. It's more than that. It requires emotional commitment on my part. You get sucked into it. In some ways it's not so good because you spend too much time, and your emotional commitment to the task is probably greater than the client's. I need a client who feels that I can supply something they want. If it's too hard-nosed my mind begins to wander and it all becomes frightfully laborious and uphill work. That doesn't turn me on.

Presumably if the client just lets you get on with it that isn't enough – you need something more positive from them? Yes, you need grit in there, a bit of interaction. You need to be close enough to be able to call him at home on a Sunday morning and say 'Look, I've got a better idea' or 'I've changed my mind, give me another couple of days.'

Do they need a little bit of the designer in them? I think they do and most of them are probably frustrated creative people. They have an interest in the process. They are capable of leaps of imagination. They also have to be risk-takers to some degree, and have a strong enough belief in themselves not to think of it as a risk. They have to have that entrepreneurial ingredient in them. If they're worried about what their boss is going to say, forget it. With a lot of them I also become good friends.

One of the things Pentagram has emphasized over the years is being outside fashion and aspiring to produce work with a 'timeless' quality so that something that works in 1975 is still applicable in 1995. The Reuters identity, for instance, has stood up well. It could have been done tomorrow, in fact.

Is timelessness an ambition? I don't think that timelessness is an ambition. It's the side-product. The solution has to be based on some aspect of the problem, not be something you stick on the problem to hide it. It's not putting lipstick on a gorilla! If that's the brief, then you redesign the gorilla, or the lipstick, or whatever. But you must have a solid idea so you can discuss the solution with the client and he can understand why you've done it that way. That's one benefit of working in a group situation: you're sharing with other like-minded people. If they say, 'We don't think that's any good' it's no good insisting 'It is', or you just end up bickering. If you say, 'I did it for these reasons', then they can say, 'Well, maybe you didn't push it far enough' or 'It's the wrong route.' It becomes a positive discussion, not just a 'I like it like this.' Actually, I'm not against that either. I quite often use that ploy. But I've got all the arguments ready in my head if they're not satisfied. If you have a solid concept, it has the potential to be timeless because it's not fixed to what's hot this month.

So the important thing to leave out is what is usually described as the stylistic element? Style is a curious word because it can mean all sorts of things, from mannerism to charisma. However, as far as I'm concerned either what you've done has panache or it hasn't. You can't design panache.

What are the qualities that distinguish a first-rate piece of work, a piece with panache, from the also-ran? It has a resonance about it, as opposed to a dull thud. You can get quite excited listening to someone describe why they did something, but when you actually look at it, it's a let-down. It doesn't have that extra quality. Take that poster on the wall which was done in 1938 [Tschichold's 'Der Berufsphotograph']. What I think is marvellous about it is that it actually has what today would be considered every cliché you could imagine. 'How can I make this photograph interesting? I'll make it negative!' It's got underlining and neat typography butted up to the edges. It's got every cliché in the book, but it still has a resonance to it. For its period it's a knockout. It still is. Tschichold was solving his own problems. He wasn't copying from someone else and re-dressing it up.

Is this intuition of quality beyond words or can you pin it down? If it can't be expressed in any way, how can we communicate it to other people? I don't think you can. Let's say you're at a party and someone walks in and you just know that there's something special about them. They have charisma. Now the more you try to pin it down and explain what it is, the worse it gets. The fact is that you just intuitively know.

Will this quality come through even if what we might call the graphic language is unfamiliar? I'm thinking here of some of the new computer-based work which is very layered and complex. Or will you need to learn a slightly different way of looking first? In the end it has nothing to do with whether it's done on a computer or that it's a very carefully laid-out piece of letterpress type. That's the means of expression, the tone of voice, the way somebody communicates. Dadaist and de Stijl typography, or Tschichold, were probably more of a break with the reigning views of their time than the computer graphic styles of today. The work of Franco Grignani or Max Huber in the 1950s is different only in degree to so-called New Wave typography. Peter Behrens was right when he said that typography is the most characteristic portrait of a period. I agree that one has to adopt a slightly different way of looking, but that's not so much of an age gap – as a habit gap. The things we now think of as 'classic' weren't necessarily viewed as such when they were first produced. Personally I find a real attraction in the iconoclastic – a kitsch object, a deconstructed building, a Dieter Rot book. Maybe your question contains its own answer. Perhaps quality is when something or someone introduces us to a new way of looking at something.

What do you mean when you say that for you design is a calling? It almost suggests a sense of apartness from everyday life. I think design is a calling. I don't mean in the ecclesiastical sense. But most people can't see with any acuity. Their eyes skid over things, but they're not really aware of what they're looking at. Take a typical person and look at the kind of furniture they have, the clothes they wear, the food they eat, the things they read – if they read – and the places they go on holiday, and you realize that they are probably missing 90 per cent of the pleasure to be got out of things because they don't really see anything. You are taught to talk, read and write, but no one seems to teach you how to perceive.

Over the years designers have talked a lot about educating the client and persuading the client to accept a higher standard of design. Have you gone about it in that almost missionary way? No. Life's too short and I don't have the patience. I don't even like teaching in art school, let alone trying to educate some client who hasn't the slightest interest. No, I'd sooner get out of there as quickly as possible. The only thing I am trying to express is how you can resolve something with freedom rather than using all those crutches: 'I have to do it this way because that's what my peers think . . . I have to do it this way because that's what I was taught . . . It really has to be done this way because that's what the client expects.' If you want to use a computer, great; if you want to put ink on the soles of a pair of shoes and dance on the paper, that's great too. You should be free to do or use whatever is appropriate.

Have you done much teaching over the years? No, but I once taught for six weeks at Yale. I was pleased to be asked. I had this vision of strolling across the Newhaven Green to the school during the morning, looking at the trees and strolling back at four. It wasn't like that at all! You walk in and 'thump!', there are all these students queuing up to question you about this and that. And I was thinking, 'Well, I've got to be very patient here.' After a few days I had a bet with myself that I could guess what the next question would be. When I began scoring eight out of ten, I realized I didn't have the patience – or skill – to teach. It was harder work than designing with little to show at the end of it – I admit it is a profound disability on my part.

You've said that one of the most salutary things about doing the book was that you realized how often you returned to earlier ideas. Yes, but I've realized that although I do that, which was a bit of a shock to me, I try to avoid just repeating something, although it happens sometimes because your back's against the wall. It's a matter of survival isn't it? But often you can take something and think, 'Well, I didn't actually do it well enough the first time' and for my own pleasure I'll do it again, because I want to add the bit I missed out the first time, or perhaps do it in a different sort of way.

You once told me you were an optimist. I was really struck, looking through the proofs of the book, just how much optimism there is in your work. You refer again and again to the good life, to wine, to restaurants, to travel, to friendship. These themes run through the imagery that attracts you and the way in which you depict it. That's because I enjoy doing it. It's a sensual, pleasurable activity. My work, like everyone else's, is a reflection of my personality. It's difficult for a designer's work to be incognito.

It's there in the 'smiling' steins you are designing for the Munich beer festival. I was trying to find something appropriate – a lot of people having a good time drinking! You don't exactly get this across with an abstract shape and a bit of Helvetica. I think the symbol should be something that people can respond to, which means you've got your thought from here to there. The best example of that is if I say something and the other person bursts out laughing or, for that matter, bursts into tears: it's immediate. Instant transfer. That's what I mean. In order to transfer a thought it has to be in a format that both parties understand.

Does that mean that the design language has to confine itself to essentially simple statements, that there's a limit to what you can say in design, that it has to be instantly transferable? I think it depends. Some 'statements' can be so simple that they don't attract attention. Others are so complicated that they don't encourage attention. I like to try to squeeze things down to their essence. There are those who prefer to make more of an orchestral arrangement. I like to make a single clear note. It's a matter of taste and inclination, not one of rules and ethics. Anything goes as long as it serves its purpose. In graphics the purpose is to transfer a thought, or information, or a sensation, from one head to another. The bait should suit the fish – not the angler.

Drawing has been really important in your recent work and there are some designers such as Milton Glaser who have argued that drawing is quite fundamental to design education and one of the problems is the way that the keyboard has replaced the drawing board. What is your own view of drawing's place in design? I used to hate going to life-drawing classes or having to render plaster casts. But that's because I was taught that drawing is done by 6H pencils. That isn't my idea of drawing, it's something else. More a matter of making pictorial notes. You don't really see something unless you draw it, or at least unless you mentally draw it. It makes you look at things. You don't have to draw very well either – which I don't – because what I actually enjoy is the sensuality of doing it.

Why has handwriting become so important in your work? It's not important, it's convenient. I once thought, 'Why take out a typebook, go through 2,000 typefaces, make up my mind whether I want it in Baskerville or Blindfish, bold or squashed? Why not just write the message down?' I also quite liked the notion of scribbling a drawing and caption as one thing. Furthermore, the combination of picture and word can often create an additional meaning.

What were you thinking of when you told me on a previous occasion that as a designer you find it hard to 'let go'? To be able to look at things in a new or different way you have to hoover preconceptions out of your mind. That's not always easy as they are often so deeply embedded that we don't recognize them as such. Even when we do there is a tendency to clutch on to them for comfort.

Is a strong personal style a strength or a weakness? If by style you mean mannerism, then I suppose it's a weakness. If you mean an unconscious expression of personality, then it's a strength. Mind you, if the personality isn't attractive – or of any interest – then I guess it's just unfortunate.

There has always been a sense with Pentagram that part of the reason it exists in the form it does is to give you all pleasant lives. Well, what do you expect? You can be a hermit, which probably has a great deal to be said for it! But surely, life is about enjoyment. If everybody concentrated on having a good time they wouldn't be arguing, or cutting each other dead in the street, or shooting each other, or whatever, because that's contrary to having a good time. What is the alternative? Having a boring or unpleasant time? Design is a style of living.

The strange thing is that while you pursued this vision large areas of British design became fairly grey in the 1980s in the attempt to become more businesslike. It became a standard job, didn't it? The implication is that you work like crazy all week

so that you can go and do something else on Saturday and Sunday. I find that odd. I'd sooner do the same on Monday or Wednesday as I do on a Saturday or Sunday. I don't divide my life between labour and pleasure.

Did the spirit go out of it somewhere between the mid-1950s, when you started, and today? Perhaps the passion of the few became diluted by the pursuit of a career by the many. You had to be out of your mind to want to be a designer in the 1950s. There were no jobs around. It was like being an actor, you knew you were going to spend most of your life washing-up. Actually I did that too – and never again if I can avoid it. It only became something people could expect to get paid for in the mid-1960s. By the mid-1970s there were squads coming out of the art schools and by the mid-1980s there were battalions. They couldn't all be doing it for the same reasons as the people who started before the 1960s. There was a different motivation.

Looking back at your career, you have made self-assured choices right from the start, like a person who knew exactly where he was going. You got yourself an education with the best people in London, went off to America and made the right connections again. Then you came back and were in at the beginning of the professionalization of graphic design in the 1960s. There is no question that it helps to be in the right place at the right time. Some times are perhaps easier than others and you don't know that until later, looking back. When I came back to London in the late 1950s, I thought I had made the worst move of my life. I remember walking round Bloomsbury. It was winter, grey and gloomy, with all those dreary offices illuminated by 40 watt bulbs. But, with hindsight, it was the right time to return because suddenly everything began to change. Bob Gill used to say it was like shooting fish in a barrel. We were raised on the survival principle. It was a period for the street-smart. Perhaps it also suggests a certain confidence. I don't know. I'm not into self-analysis. I might clog up my intuition if I did. Self-questioning is something else – that's what drives me. If you're not questioning yourself, you're just trotting out experiences and going around in circles. But I don't think about these kind of things too much. I am intent on discovering who I am, and I do what I do.

Overleaf

This is a selection of graphic observations drawn for the owner of three fine intimate hotels and a restaurant in London. The hotelier explained that he worked hard at promoting his hotels, and every evening, when abroad on business, would buy postcards to send to everyone he had seen during that day. He wanted a series of postcards to capture the warmth, hospitality and ambience of his hotels. So Fletcher spent a day visiting them, drawing vignettes of the people, and the flowers and the antiques found in each place. The narrative wit demonstrates how, as in much of his work, word and picture are inseparable.

sketch of The Dorset Square Hotel

we serve flowers
for breakfast and
lunch and dinner.

a dialogue between two chairs
at the Pelham Hotel

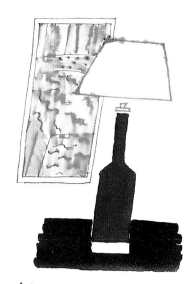

reflection in a mirror
of a Queen size bed in
room 202 at The Pelham.

Emma and apples —
Reception desk at the Pelham

The barman at the
Dorset Square Hotel
about to deliver
a bodyliner.

There's a reason why they
keep cricket bats in the
umbrella stand at The
Dorset Square Hotel—
next time you stay there
— ask them.

A blue rinse tête-à-tête
at the Dorset Square Hotel

The art of making four pointed
stars out of square cushions

Portrait of a guest

A rendez vous

WHAT
DISTINGUISHES
DESIGNER SHEEP
FROM
DESIGNER GOATS
IS THE ABILITY
TO STROKE
A CLICHÉ
UNTIL IT PURRS
LIKE
A METAPHOR

AF

Body language

Artists have been depicting parts of the human body for thousands of years. Inevitably mouths, hearts and hands have become visual clichés, but in Fletcher's work they are used in different and unexpected ways, and become icons in their own right.

The amorphous figure illustrated here is of a man gearing up to leap into the next millennium, a poster image for the 'World City Expo' held in Tokyo in 1996. This section examines a few of his other playful interpretations of human features.

when I'm good
I'm very good
but when I'm bad
— I'm better.

Mae West

One aspect of Fletcher's work is that he will develop the same subject, extending its use and refining its execution over several different jobs. When asked to create a sign for the reception area of a new design office, Fletcher produced a wicked, welcoming smile. Afterwards, however, the drawing troubled him – it looked indecisive. The issue, as he saw it, was that 'I was trying to draw lips rather than making marks to represent a smile'. For a poster which illustrated the famous quip by Mae West he did just that, and produced a salacious smile.

Although he could sometimes be accused of applying a predetermined solution, he will only do so if he feels it is appropriate. In his solution for a poster produced by London Transport to encourage the public to travel by bus, he created a collection of animated and chattering mouths to represent a cocktail party. Once again, he characteristically set himself a new goal – to see if he could convey several different personalities.

As a graphic symbol, the heart shape has a relatively short visual history – compared to, say, the eye. The Valentine shown on the left plays on duplication: what remains when you remove the heart is also a heart, an apt configuration in the context of love and loss.

This calligraphic design was produced for Dauphin who own poster and billboard sites throughout France. To celebrate the 48th anniversary of the Cannes Film Festival, they held an exhibition of posters especially commissioned from designers around the world. The theme was to design a poster for a classical film, which had been made in their respective countries.

The blotchy effect of the image was achieved by writing the title in ink directly onto blotting paper. The final design was reproduced in white on a black background.

Handprints

The earliest form of personal identity is the prehistoric handprint. When an entrepreneurial bill poster in Munich persuaded the city authorities to mount an exhibition of public art on the cylindrical street hoardings, Fletcher's contribution echoed the ancient practice when he produced a black-and-white poster of his own handprints. His ambition was to encourage pedestrians to add their own mucky prints and so enrich the pattern.

He returned to the same theme for a poster announcing an exhibition at the Design Museum in London. Achieving the colourful handprint posed problems from the start. He didn't have any printing inks and so tried acrylics, but these didn't prove satisfactory. So then he resurrected the black-and-white handprint originally used for Munich, squidged different colours onto an overlay, and sent it off to be proofed. He wanted to see the effect before embarking on a trip to the printer to do it properly. He admits to occasional laziness.

When the proof was returned, he thought it more interesting than if it had been done in the way originally intended. So he used it exactly as it had been proofed. The print has one flaw, however. The stigmata are perhaps more the result of carelessness than of any other intention.

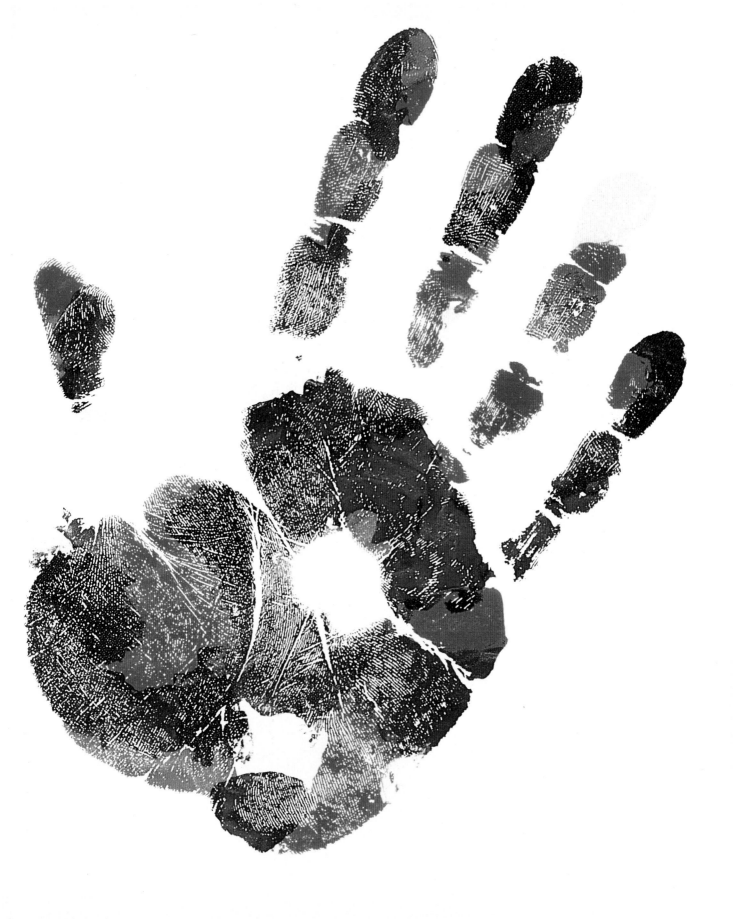

CARING FOR THE EARTH AND ITS PEOPLE

The blue hand was produced to promote a design seminar at which there were six keynote speakers. Many people don't immediately make the connection. Fletcher traced an outline of his own hand, simply shifting it to gain the extra finger, and then filled it in. The outline is exposed at odd points to reveal the process, because, he says, 'a deliberate imperfection can often disguise the involuntary ones.'

The introduction of the little finger supporting the globe in a design for a World Conservation conference in Argentina would, he thought, imply a more delicate balance than using the index finger. He found it in a manual illustrating hand sign language: it actually means the letter J.

Often Alan Fletcher seems to deliberately flirt with clichés, perhaps because, so he says, 'it helps if you have something to work against'. For instance a poster for Observatoire Internationale des Prisons, an organization dedicated to the rights of prison inmates, employs the graphic trick of enlarging a printed photograph to produce a texture of dots. But in this case the dots are not mechanically reproduced, but laboriously rendered by hand on cheap brown wrapping paper (a material chosen to suggest the utilitarian existence of prisoners). Seen close up, the poster appears to be abstract, but viewed from a distance it reveals part of a face, and the hidden but watchful eye of the organization. A cliché of a cliché of a cliché.

This ubiquitous thumbprint was used to represent the complexities inherent in corporate identity. But in this instance the cliché is converted into a metaphor. It is not an actual imprint of his thumb but a copy, carefully drawn, line by line, in pencil – a matter of drawing one's own identity.

The face opposite appeared on a poster to promote
Kindersdorf villages. These are family communities
which adopt and foster orphans and deprived children.
The characteristic of the poster is that the whole
sheet of paper represents the face and simply adding
childlike marks creates the features (also see page 206).

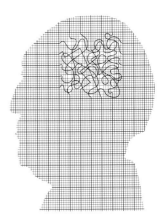

The portrait in the advertisement (above) was achieved
by extracting the relevant page from the magazine and
carefully folding it to make a face. In this case the logotype
on the masthead supplied the features.

The head on the right expresses the notion that design
is a plan to make something. The self portrait on the left
says what it is.

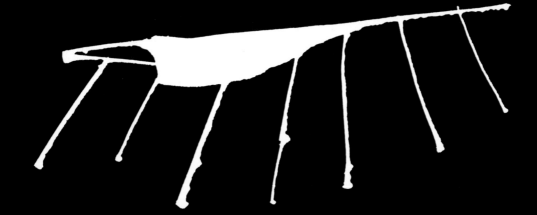

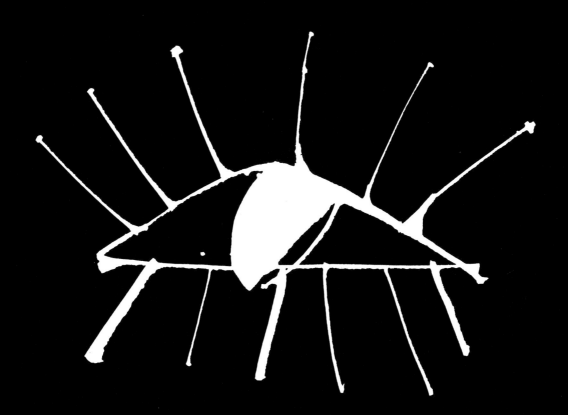

I once presented a complex design project to a client who had offices in Hamburg and Milan.

I arrived at the German office and was ushered into the boardroom to confront a dozen seriously grey suits.

Everyone was introduced to everyone else and promptly sat down.

I unzipped the folio and turned to the first page which displayed the brief.

Everybody nodded.

Having set the scene I meticulously and sequentially took them through each page from initial sketches to finished design.

They looked satisfied, shook my hand, and ushered me out.

The next day I arrived in Milan.

Had a chat with the executives over espresso and unzipped the presentation.

I showed the first page to remind them of the brief.

They looked blank.

After turning over the pages, explaining this and that, I noticed they'd begun to fidget.

My cultural vibes registered . . .

I shut the folio and turned it around.

Then, opening it onto the last page which illustrated the final design, and referring dismissively to the previous pages,

enthusiastically showed the solution.

Bravo.   We all sat down to another espresso.

There are courses for horses.   AF

Alan Fletcher has been associated with the corporate symbols of some of the most visible organizations in the world. This section looks at the thinking behind the creation of marks and the attributes which make them distinctive, memorable and effective.

The designs demonstrate a wide visual vocabulary, including the pictorial language of metaphor, anagrams and palindromes. They also illustrate the categories to which identity marks belong, and the sources of the ideas behind them. 'As legibility is to words, logobility is to trademarks,' he says, then goes on to explain that, 'Logobility is the capacity of a word to be converted into a unique typographic device.'

A mark of identity should not merely be a superficial configuration but emanate directly from the personality and activity of the organization it represents. As with the Lloyd's of London logotype, which was derived from letters on a commemorative plaque by Reynolds Stone, he usually hits the mark.

The unique ingredient

Making a mark on a large organization requires skill and stamina. Reuters was Alan Fletcher's first large-scale corporate identity project (1965) and the Institute of Directors, the most recent (1994). Although there is a thirty year span between them, the two projects demonstrate that a symbol must always have a unique ingredient which somehow summarizes the essence of the organization it represents.

Gerald Long of Reuters, the international news agency, was one of those exceptional patrons of design who just don't appear to exist any more. He commissioned the proto-Pentagram team to refashion the entire organization: Fletcher had the task of creating a new logotype, Kenneth Grange designed new monitors, Mervyn Kurlansky designed the literature, and Theo Crosby designed their furniture, interiors and offices. While on a fact-finding tour of Reuters, Fletcher had watched news information coming through tickertape machines, such was the technology in those days. He put a piece of punched tape in his pocket. Back at the studio, this memento of his visit presented the solution.

The Institute of Directors decided it had to broaden its appeal and attract new members but felt that their existing graphic identity made it look more like a smart provincial engineering firm than an influential national organization. The brief listed those not untypical conflicts: 'modern but traditional', 'dynamic but conservative' and so on. The solution, reflecting the spirit of the brief, centred on adopting a traditional form but treating it unconventionally. He went about it by proportionally enlarging three letters of the same typeface into three different sizes, and then fitting them together into a monogram. The larger size of the D emphasizes Director, thus distinguishing this particular Institute from all the other Institutes.

INSTITUTE OF DIRECTORS

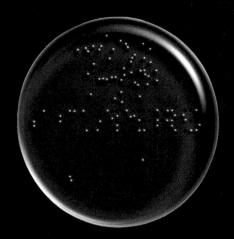

A good corporate mark is able to work in a variety of scales, from a lapel pin to a neon supersign. It should be possible to make it in a variety of materials ranging from steel to wood and to reproduce it using a variety of techniques from engraving to sky writing. In addition it needs to perform not just on standard applications such as stationery, commercial literature, vehicles and signs, but also in more peripheral circumstances.

One of the more unusual applications of the Reuters logotype was as an executive gift, devised, said Fletcher, 'to send executives demented'. This is a game in which ballbearings need to be dexterously manoeuvred into holes to reveal the name. The Institute of Directors monogram is easily adaptable as a repeat pattern: ideal for ties and scarves.

An interlocking pair of letters designed in 1969 for a sign company comprised the initials of Wilson Walton. When Mr Wilson died (we don't know what happened to Mr Walton) the company was taken over by John Wood and his family, and renamed Wood & Wood – fortuitously, as they kept the symbol. This is their neon sign.

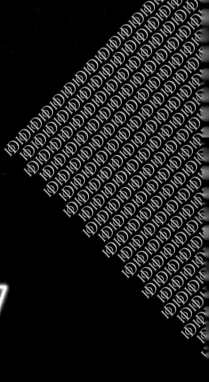

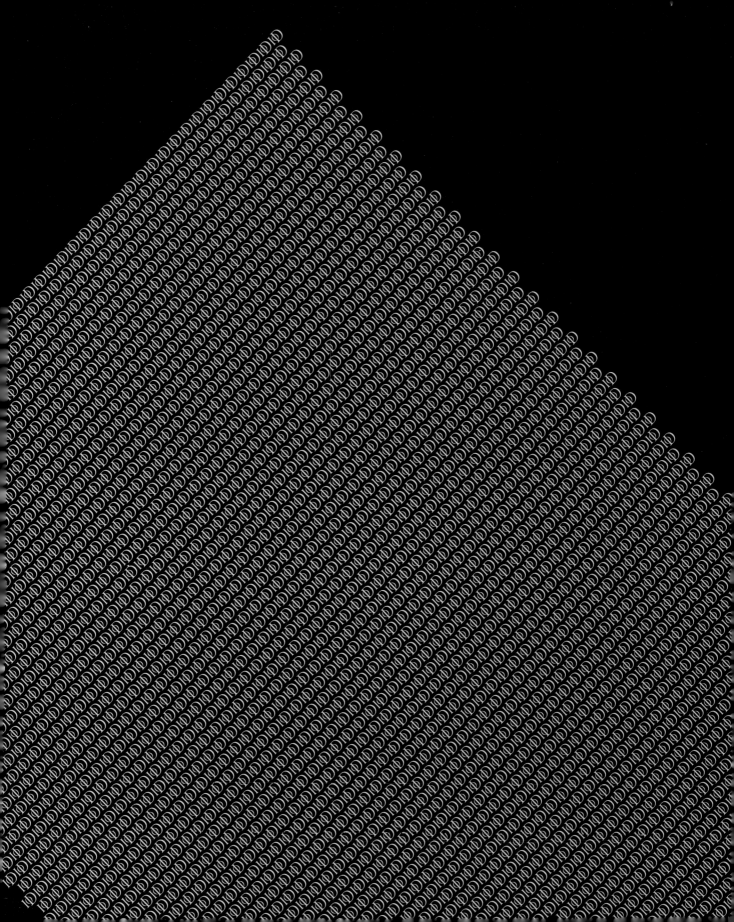

Different symbols can be categorized into different families. There are trademarks which are typographic treatments: Coca Cola and Pirelli. There are those which comprise initials, such as IBM or the swash M of MacDonalds. Some integrate a name with a picture, for example Shell. Others are abstract, such as the Chase Manhattan Bank or British Rail. A fifth category are entirely pictorial, such as Apple's apple.

The logotype for the Design Council, originally set up by Churchill's government as the Council of Industrial Design, was designed in 1978. This is an example of a typographic treatment. Gill Extra Bold was used to express 'design' boldly, sandwiched by a sense of the tradition embodied in Baskerville. Both are English typefaces. There are Scotch rules and the house colour is a vibrant Welsh red. But where is the Irish element ? 'Perhaps Design Council policy?' suggests Fletcher. The definition of a successful symbol is that it becomes synonymous with the body it represents. That's what happened in this case. When the organization decided to undertake a radical restructuring (in 1994) they judiciously decided to create a new identity.

The device for a property development in London's Chelsea Harbour is an example of how a name can be integrated with a graphic. In this case the graphics are a stencilled boat and a lifebelt. The choice of a stencil was a useful way of silhouetting the Thames spritsail barge (insisted upon by the client), and proved to be an easy method for quickly applying the design to the building site.

Industrial giants Asea of Sweden and Brown Boveri of Germany merged to form a vast multinational

conglomerate. As nobody engineering the merger could make up their minds whether it should be called AB or BAB or ABB or BBA, Fletcher and his team at Pentagram had to keep generating sketch designs to help them take a decision. Eventually the chief settled on ABB. His brief: 'I want a group of initials like IBM, and I want it in a fortnight.'

Returning from Stockholm, whilst on the plane with the clock ticking towards the deadline, he worked on two solutions. The first was an elegant composition of superimposed letters, and the second, initials divided into four to signify the four areas of corporate activity. It came as no surprise that they chose the second, more obvious solution. 'I see this logotype in every airport I ever go through,' laments Fletcher. 'It's more publicly visible than anything I've ever done and I probably like it the least.' Anyway here it is again.

The mark for an organization seeking to forge closer links between Muslim nations is an example of the abstract. The crescents, an Islamic emblem, represent the six participating countries. Fitted together, they imply unity. They are also reminiscent of the pattern visible in the twisted silk cord which encircles the Arabic head-dress.

Finally, the symbol for Escargot Productions (right) represents the pictorial family. A brushstroke with penned additions produced a snail, albeit one which looks like a prehistoric pictogram. The association is not irrelevant. The spiral, the most ancient of symbols, and the snail has always had a mystical significance: thousands were discovered buried around Stonehenge and other ancient sites.

You don't need to add decorative elements to create distinctive devices. These four examples of 'less-is-more' owe their solutions to supreme typographic economy, in which deft interventions convert letters into symbols which are exclusive to the bodies they represent.

ANNA

eva

MICHĒLE

Anna was Alan Fletcher's first assistant in 1959. He decided to design her a name style by using wood type inked and pressed on paper, which in turn was folded and pressed again to obtain a transfer. The result – a visual palindrome – is a word which can be read in either direction. A mark for a printer, Eva, is a visual anagram, the 'e' turned upside-down to create a lower case letter 'a'. Michéle, a brand name for the teenage cosmetics marketed by Marks & Spencer, acquired an accent by cutting and lifting the bar of the E.

The already classic symbol for the Victoria & Albert Museum (designed in 1989) is in a typeface originally designed by Giambattista Bodoni. The problem centred on endowing the three characters with a single personality. The solution was to divide and remove half of one letter, and add and insert an ampersand to reinstate the missing crossbar.

MILLERFESTIVAL BATH 1977

Sometimes putting two disparate elements together
can create a third entity. An emblem (right) for the
Stravinsky Festival Trust led to the visual connection
between a classical calligraphic S and a musical treble
clef. A symbol for the joiner, Mr Purser, who put
up shelving in the first studio of Fletcher Forbes Gill,
integrates a dovetail with the letter P. The joiner had
asked Fletcher what he did for a living – the intention
of the symbol was to show him. The year was 1962.
An organization founded to promote Islamic culture
was called Al Foulk, which translates as The Ark. The
horizontal bar of the letter was extended and printed
in blue to represent the flood. The apex represents
Mount Arafat, on which the Ark came to rest. Herman
Miller is an American manufacturer of classical modern
furniture and office systems by renowned designers.
They hold an annual summer garden party which they
call Millerfest. A manipulation created a sunny emblem
appropriate to the occasion. Such connections may
seem obvious in hindsight, but the skill lies in having
the foresight to perceive them in the first place.

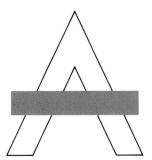

There are many graphic, pictorial and visual languages
– heraldry, semaphore, pictograms, handsigns and so on.
These are the essentials of the designer's vocabulary.

This star for the Commercial Bank of Kuwait was
constructed from a written language. The starting-point
was two words in Arabic script. The word top left reads
'commercial' and the one on the right is 'bank'. These
were written in Kufic, a geometric Arabic script, and
shaped into a component which could be assembled
into a star. This star can literally be read by Arabic
speakers and can also be easily recognized through its
pattern by non-Arabs. One doesn't have to understand
the language to comprehend the identity.

The emblem (opposite) was for Flagship Portsmouth,
a representative body for the various Trusts within the
historical naval dockyard of Portsmouth, among them
Nelson's flagship HMS Victory and the Mary Rose.
Naval flags from the International Code of Signals are
combined to make a 'P', to represent Portsmouth, and
also spell out 'A Naval History'. The flags were chosen
because of their association with things marine and
celebratory and because they could be used to spell out
promotional messages. A housestyle with a vocabulary.

Scratching around

Alan Fletcher strayed unwittingly into a politically sensitive arena when Vienna and Budapest decided to stage jointly an Expo on the Danube, so reviving the old Austro-Hungarian cultural axis. Initially the organizers held a competition to find a symbol. But, disappointed by the poor entries, they invited three international designers to present recommendations.

Fletcher's proposal was selected. The brief called for a 'culture' mark rather than a 'commercial' symbol. He investigated various routes (some of the sketches are shown here), until he settled on the final design. This unites two arrows, representing Vienna and Budapest, to make the letter X.

But in Vienna, on the eve of signing a five-year contract to design all the graphic materials, he watched the television results of a referendum. The Viennese voted to withdraw from the Expo. The project disappeared overnight. However, the Hungarians decided to continue. They requested modifications. They wanted the colours to be changed, they didn't want the symbol to be angled, they wanted '95 to be replaced with '96, they wanted amendments to the letters. He revised the designs accordingly. Eventually the Hungarians also cancelled Expo. As Fletcher commented, 'I have a lot of my solutions rejected, but to lose out on what had been accepted was a new twist.'

Overleaf

A design to celebrate fifty years of the National Gallery of Art in Washington DC takes the fifty stars out of the American flag and reassembles them to spell fifty. Well, if that seems obvious, how many stripes are there in the American flag? We take some things so for granted that we don't see them.

Wit makes connections

no⁄one thought of in

quite the same way before.

Wit exposes a likeness

in things that are different,

and a difference in things

that are alike.

Wit makes sense

out of nonsense.

Alan Fletcher has been collecting printed ephemera for years: tickets to a memorable exhibition, baggage stickers for a trip to America, an envelope from a kind letter he received – the kind of material that holds meanings for him and nobody else.

This section looks at how he puts this material to use and how in one particular project, just to make things more challenging, he imposed irrational constraints on the way it could be handled. The brief was for a calendar illustrating the Chinese horoscope, and as you see – whether a monkey or a dog – nothing goes to waste.

The dragon below is the only mythological animal amongst the twelve animals of the horoscope – and as dragons have no natural features, the most difficult. Taking a Chinese festival dragon mask as the main reference, you can discern crate labels to indicate breathing fire (see also page 169), a Rolodex file card to make the fangs and Fletcher's first motor tax disc.

For these Chinese horoscope animals, consider the self-imposed constraints and think about whether they reach new levels of self-discipline, arrogance, stupidity or perhaps insight. For instance, he decided to restrict himself to the animal heads. To confine his palette to his collection of ephemera. And, to make things even harder, to employ no other techniques. Working within the narrow limitations prescribed, each animal had to be brought to life.

It was only when the project started that he realized the task he'd set for himself. A snake, for instance, doesn't really have a head. An ox's head is hardly very familiar. Once a likeness had been achieved by assembling and reassembling the materials, the heads were composed by meticulously lining up the edges of papers, picking up typographic relationships and juxtaposing colours and textures.

The collages also use personal references, asides and recollections, such as an airmail envelope which once held a letter from André François or one of his mother-in-law's tarot cards. Much of the material used is of historical interest, such as the BOAC airline tickets. One gets a brief glimpse of his lifestyle in the tickets for the Venice Biennale or the voucher for the New York La Guardia Airport Skycap service. And just what did he see at the Royal Court Theatre on 16th January 1960? Whatever production it was, you couldn't get in for 16 shillings today.

Some people can't see the animals, let alone recognize them. But many can. And for them, perhaps, the most sublime touch lies in using the black stripe on the back of a British Rail ticket to denote the monkey's mouth.

The Ox

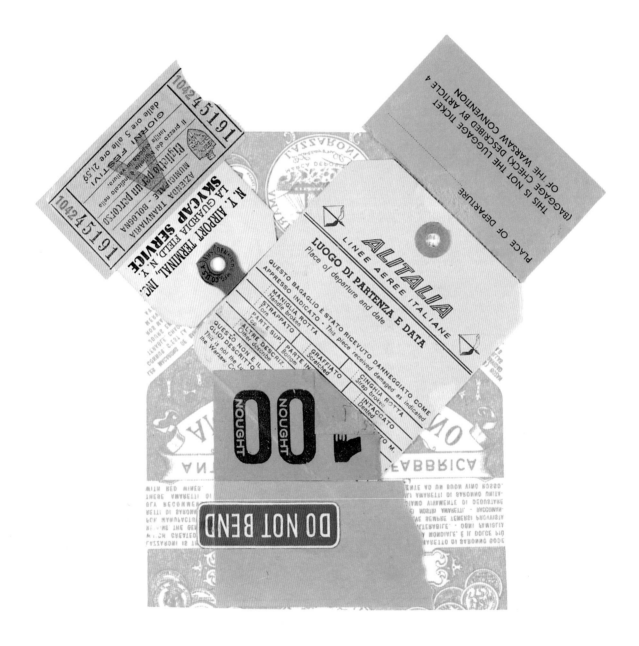

spaper
eeds
e tags
Many
ntries,
an be

You've got to have

<u>the courage</u>

to close your eyes

and jump in the dark

aware that you may

land on your face

and have to get up

SMILING

After all, you're going to have to do it again tomorrow.

AF

This section looks at Fletcher's talent for manipulating perceptions. Some of the examples have been adapted from those used by perceptual psychologists; others he has generated himself. These eye-teasing tricks with perspective and visual ambiguity may look simple, but that's part of the art.

As with the two chairs (on page 119), which he noticed while lying on a beach in Greece, some scenes contain more than immediately meets the eye. In this case by slightly moving his head the stacked chairs could be bisected by the horizon. The implication was obvious. He didn't need to test it by standing on his head.

His observations of unexpected balances, encounters, or collisions, have their repercussions in his designs. Such visual conundrums hold his fascination and fuel the amusement of finding unusual solutions to prosaic problems.

Although the emblem for the International Society for Heart Research is flat and linear, the pattern implies it is spherical. A demonstration that two dimensions can make three.

The Z for the Zinc Development Association appears three-dimensional but analyze it and you will discover it is an impossible proposition. Trench becomes wall. The design amalgamates both positive and negative to represent the dual forms of a zinc die-casting mould.

The illusion which conjures up a glass of Beaujolais presented itself over a drink one evening. The two-dimensional implies the three-dimensional, the wine glass is made to stand up. A case of I drink therefore I am, or less is more than enough.

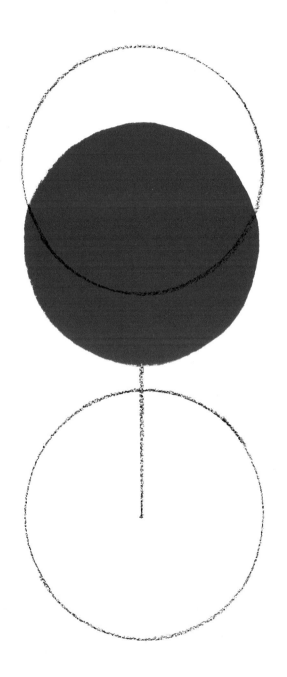

The visual paradox makes one think twice, and thus it becomes more memorable. Asked to design an emblem for advertising agency Manton Woodyer and Ketley, Fletcher constructed the intriguing visual illusion (below). Are the flowers in the picture frame or in a vase on the table in front of the frame? The illusion could be viewed as a wry comment on advertising agencies – all smoke and mirrors! But the flowers, which are taken from a Victorian scrapbook, also look like an owl and owls are wise. Incidentally the design was physically set up in the agency's reception but they kept forgetting to change the flowers, which rather spoilt the effect.

A similar ambiguity can be found in an evocation of Wimbledon, which appeared on a calendar on the page for June. The shadow leaves the question of which side of the line the tennis ball has fallen on – always a controversial one – unanswered.

Overleaf

The following pages show some other examples of 'now you see it, now you don't'. An invitation card to celebrate a birthday, a holiday sketch, a symbol for a civil engineering company, a design for a menu and wine list, a picture of a friend's dog.

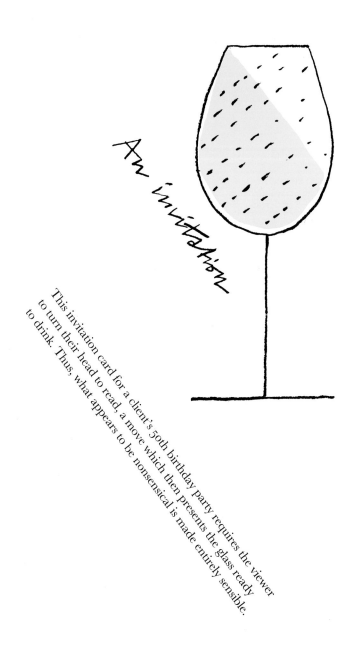

An invitation

This invitation card for a client's 50th birthday party requires the viewer to turn their head to read, a move which then presents the glass ready to drink. Thus, what appears to be nonsensical is made entirely sensible.

Red chair on a blue chair

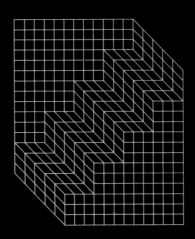

Illusionist

Optimist

Pessimist

Rationalist

Dog

Received a call from a multinational corporation to attend a briefing in Holland. We have a company plane, they explained, that will be ready to leave Gatwick at 8.30am on Monday morning. 'Be there'. Staggered out of bed at 5.00am, too late for coffee, took a taxi to Victoria Station, a train to Gatwick, arrived at the check-in desk, was whisked off to a mini-bus, and arrived at the open door of an eight-seater corporate jet. A hostess with clipboard raised a smile and asked my name. 'Odd', she said, 'there are already two on board with that name and the plane is full.' The explanation was overbooking. Someone had assumed there was only one Fletcher, and that the three different Fletchers were one and the same. Returned to the terminal, the train, the taxi and got home for breakfast. Phone call to the client. Sorry, and all that, come tomorrow on a regular flight. 'Be in Eindhoven at 2pm.'

Up again at 5.00am, too late for coffee. Taxi to Heathrow, ran to check-in desk, rushed off to plane. 'Sorry' announced the air hostess, 'no coffee – it's only a short hop'. Rushed from plane to taxi. Was deposited at Rotterdam railway station. Bar open but train just about to leave. Into train – no buffet. Arrived at Eindhoven, saw café but was running late. Jumped into taxi. Arrived at headquarters. Conducted up to executive boardroom full of replete suits (it was just after lunch) finishing cigars over empty coffee cups. They got down to business. Once finished it was pointed out that I could make the last flight back to London – if I was quick. Down in the elevator, into a taxi to the station....you've got the story. Arrived home after midnight. Had a strong coffee. Couldn't sleep all night. And swore never to travel more than 50 miles without staying the night, or leaving the previous day, at the client's expense. Incidentally – I never got the job. AF

A pictorial tour of the twelve countries of the European Community for a calendar is the subject of this section. The task of representing each of the countries could have been tackled in a variety of ways. Fruit, flowers and vegetables presented an early option – from Dutch tulips to Brussel sprouts. Other subjects such as Danish bicycles and Portuguese men-of-war crowded into his mind as he juggled with concepts. Some of these early sketches are shown on page 136.

Fletcher's method is to cut down the options steadily, settle on one route, and then fix constraints into both subject and technique until the essence can be defined and its execution achieved. In this case, he decided to search for a single theme that could be interpreted in twelve ways, rather than an *ad hoc* assembly of disparate approaches. The theme he settled on was landscapes – or at least various aspects of landscapes. Each one takes a different view and a written caption helps make the mental jump and thus put the graphic in context.

The toughest subject was Luxembourg; 'A big name for a small place,' he thought. Remembering that a girl at Pentagram came from there, he asked her to give him some suggestions. She icily responded that she was from Lichtenstein. He finally looked it up in *Pears Cyclopedia*. This said that Luxembourg was a small country of hills and valleys. As that's what it said, that's what he wrote.

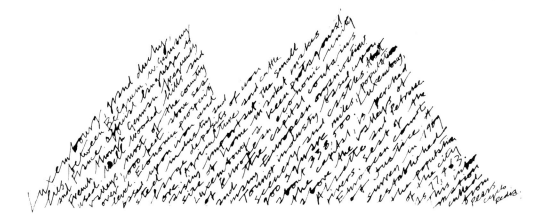

Scenarios

Three of the scenes shown on the following pages use old, scuffed and distressed industrial coloured tapes. Apparently they were lying around the studio. How he made the connection between industrial tape and flags, or seascape and canals, is not quite so easy to explain – intuition perhaps?

Just as Fletcher was pondering on a solution for France, he went to a Raoul Dufy exhibition. The festive scenes, often full of flags, triggered the thought of a *Jour de fête*. A joyful assembly of tricolours, or rather red and blue tape. Note that the white stripe is implied, not shown.

The depiction of 'Ireland as seen from Wales' is also deceptively simple, but it belies its execution. The flick of a pencil produces the whiplash of rain. The white capped waves of the sea were arrived at by scratching printed grey paper with a scalpel. The black strokes and white scratches in turn tonally affect the single grey which is made to appear as two different greys.

A plan of Amsterdam suggested a design based on an aerial view, with blue tape used to represent the grid of canals and a page taken from a telephone directory to signify the buildings. He asked a Dutch friend to tear from the Amsterdam directory the page which had the address of his old friend, Wim Crouwel, self-styled master of graphic functionalism. The design makes more than a passing nod to Mondrian's 1943 painting, *Boogie Woogie*, showing Manhattan as seen from the top of a skyscraper. 'I knew there would be nothing Wim would like less than a sloppy Mondrian,' said Fletcher mischievously. And sent him the calendar.

jour de fête

Amsterdam...a sloppy Mondrian

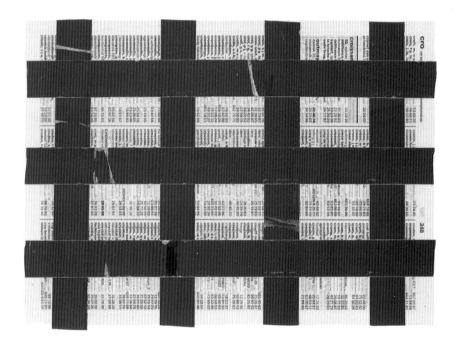

Ireland…as seen from Wales

A Greek island

Greece is represented by the memory of a summer holiday spent on a particularly arid, hot island. Torn brown wrapping paper – its grain reflecting a rocky terrain – sits beneath the most prickly, aggressive sun Fletcher could draw. Pushing this a step further, the sun was printed in fiery fluorescent orange to convey a sense of searing heat.

The German landscape on the next page parodies a national trait of uniformity by depicting the Black Forest as imprecise trees on a precise grid. Each tree was scrawled out with the cap dispenser of a bottle of Indian ink – a poignant reference to acid rain and a vivid reminder of his reliance on an uncontrolled technique to achieve an unpredictable result.

The scene for Belgium is inspired by Poppy Day, when the war dead are commemorated in Britain with the wearing of a red paper poppy in the lapel. A symbol to recall the death and destruction in World War I in the fields of Flanders. The landscape is made to recede into the distance as the flowers gradually diminish in shape and size.

The glow of sunburnt bodies on a crowded beach on the Spanish Costa Brava was achieved by printing in bronze metallic ink. The human figures (and one dog drawn in a convenient space) remain the same size but distance is implied as the figures are cut off at the ankles and waist as they apparently go into the sea.

A field in Flanders

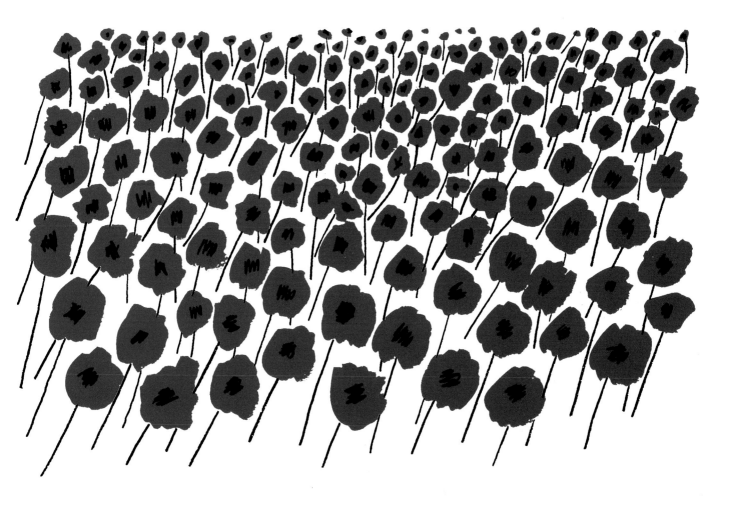

Some preliminary sketches

Brussel sprouts

Luxembourg —
...une for a small p...

Copenha...

Portuguese
Sardines

Fletcher's visual interpretations of different countries are reflected in one of his best-known and most useful innovations. He has his favourite places to visit. And his favourite places have become ours because he has created a unique international information network about the attractions to be found in cities around the world. Feedback is a series of Pentagram booklets, distributed to clients, colleagues and friends, which began in the 1980s. Inside each edition (which appears every four or five years), designers, artists, architects, writers and photographers give descriptions of the most interesting hotels, restaurants, street markets, shops, theatres, galleries, etc they have encountered on their recent business travels.

He attributes his decision to launch Feedback to one cold, rainy winter night in Hamburg. He had arrived there on a Sunday evening as he had an early meeting on Monday morning, but he didn't fancy dining in the empty hotel restaurant. He asked the concierge to recommend another and was directed to one which on arrival he found equally drab and gloomy. He deeply regretted not having asked a local designer beforehand where an interesting restaurant could be located on a Sunday night in February.

Then the thought occurred to him. Many designers travelling abroad on business must find themselves in the same fix. Fletcher wrote to his contacts in the creative community, requesting recommendations on what to do, where to eat and where to stay in the world's major cities. Slowly the feedback trickled in – postcards from Tahiti, letters from Milan, notes on the back of menus from New York, all describing architectural delights and culinary treats well off the tourist track. Today Feedback is an institution. There are quite a few designers who refuse to leave for the airport without the latest edition packed in their case.

FEEDBACK is put together and published by Pentagram with the help of their friends.

Artists, designers, writers, architects and photographers have a unique advantage in that they belong to an international fraternity. And when travelling to unfamiliar cities, and as to where to go, are often taken by a friend or colleague to an interesting corner of the city.

We asked contributors to restrict their recommendations to major cities, but have also included a few exotic locations as these might prove worth a detour between airports. Although every effort has been made to check the descriptions and addresses, changes inevitably occur. We welcome corrections or comments for future editions.

Alan Fletcher, Pentagram 1992.

buy it bottled as there is no ...
Beware, it can be addictive (in ...
Bob Brooks, Film Director, Lond...

Barcelona, Catalunya

My favourite places in Barcelona:
El Tragaluz Restaurant-Bar
Passage de la Concepcio 5, 08008 Ba...
Tel: (343) 487 0621
La Sala Vinçon Art Gallery
Paseo de Gracia 96. Tel: (343) 215 6050
Philippe Starck, Designer, Paris

Vinçon
If you want to buy the most charming kitchen ...
all you need to do is catch a plane and make fo...
You take a taxi ... address, Passeig de...
The ... household articles, ...
... ks, everything you ca...
... without snobbery, of l...
... gent, unusual, differe...
... er of...
Th...

Mount...
Victorian ...
Preserve. It offe...
rock climbing, hiking ...
have a meeting, a confere...
are faintly reminiscent of an E...
serve a nice tea in the aftern...
in public and bedrooms. Ra...
Jon Naar, Photographer, Ne...

New York

Petrel Sailing
Foot of Battery Park. Tel ...
Take a sail around lower ...
yawl built in the Thirties ...
unforgettable (especial...
R O Blechman, Illustra...

Basta Pasta
37 West 17th Street ...
Who better to make ...
Japanese. After all ...
Fiat and Ford. Bas...
York branch of a ...
food. Obsessive ...
servient service ...
Tibor Kalman, D...

George's Voo
South 4th Stre...
Williamsburg ...
Whatever yo...
old one, to g...
you a voodo...
he usually o...
wallet whe...
your fee...
with a se...
Lo...

large table o...
can imagine. Absolute ...
bakery school which obviously ...
bread being served above. Some an...
the form of chocolate sculptures ar...
acts are on display on the lower le...
Steff Geissbuhler, Designer, New ...

Meggen

Hotel Angelfluh
Ch-6045 Meggen (near Lucer...
You could get to this wonde...
in almost 10 minutes from ...
Italian and fish dishes!' If i...
the lake side. The house h...
surroundings are absolut...
have also rooms to stay ...
*Try once their 'gourm...
Josef Müller-Brockman...

Hôtel de So...
1833 Les Avants...
Have you ever re...
take the famous ...
Les Avants. The ...
overlooking ...
there - at 1,2...
genuine 19th ...
castle. All ...
unique alp...
discreet s...
nights...
Thierry ...

Nikos ...
462 A...
The b...
tortur...
and ...
fro...

Phoenix,

Tee Pee Re...
Indian Schoo... Tel:...
A fun and funky Mexican ...
inexpensive (TexMex) foo...
find it listed in any touri...
very popular with local ...
crowded and noisy. ...
Richard Danne, Desi...

Lunch at L'Aube...
89A Oak Creek, P...
When visiting Ph...
see the incredi...
and the Painted Desert ...
is a town surrounded comp...
cliffs of fantastic shapes. ...
Wayne movies, and it's br...
group of log cabins and ...
Sit outside, order some ...
at the cliffs. It's all very ...
Paula Scher, Designer, ...

The Heard Museum
22 E. Monte Vista Roa...
The Heard Museum is ...
west Indian Art anywh...
and superbly simple. ...
to while driving throu...
Deborah Sussman, Desi...

Arcosanti, north o...
... eri's City ...

156
158

Sapinta, Maramures County

Rumania

Merry Cemetery
Situated in the remote village of Sapinta, close to the Ukrainian border, is one of the most unique examples of East European folk art. The Merry Cemetery's colourfully painted carved wooden grave markers created by Stan Patras in 1935, depict scenes from the life, or the disaster which led to the death of the deceased, accompanied by humorous epitaphs.
Arnold Schwartzman, Filmmaker & Designer, Los Angeles

Leningrad

Russia

Restaurant Kavkazkij
Prospettiva Nevskij 25, Leningrad. Tel: 311 39 77
A very charming restaurant for its wooden interior decorated with its Georgian atmosphere and its large wall paintings. Patronized by few tourists and by many Caucasians who have come north. Typical cuisine with courses like mutton skewers, chicken in walnut sauce, beans with onions, vinegar-g... other deliciousness difficult to describe. There are t... kind waiters, Arkadij and Sergej (who is the waiter ... to be contacted for reservations). It is advisabl... otherwise you may not find place. Also advisab... porter (1$), or you will find it hard to reach Se... reservations. The nicest room is the last one ...
Tullio Pericoli, Illustrator, Milan

Moscow

Tolstoy House Museum
21 Lev Tolstoy Street, (Ulitsa L'va To...
Don't bother to go to the dull and ...
Instead, take a taxi to the writer's ...
building in a run-down bit of Mos...
as it must have done in Tolsto...
wrote; the big diningroom tav...
where Mme Tolstoy receive...
where the governess taug...
neglected warren of chil...
never did up; and the o...
meals. Visited by pan...
or two scholars, bu...
getting there.
David Gentleman ...

The Melnikov ...
Krivoarbatsk...
Alongside ...
All tourist...

Bern

Switzerla...

Restaurant du Theatre - Theaterplatz and
Restaurant Romantique Lowen
Worb (near Bern)
Kurt Wirth, Designer, Bern

Klosters

Switzerl...

... el
... ternatio...
... comb, fit ...
... bathroom ...
scene on ...
... ellous, truly ...
... n language ...
... dering can ...
Store' is ...
... signer, He...

... nghai:
Top floor ...
: North B...
es/coolth ...
od). Nort...
ing/Sha...
nghai OI...
beside ...
uses als...
three ne...
... r Smith ...

Ristorante C...
Hammerstrass...
An Italian restau...
... phere. Always cro...
Olle Eksell, Designe...

Gasthaus zum Hirsc...
Egerten. Tel: (06926) 3...
Aigle
Folgensbourg. Tel: (068) 6...
About ten miles on the lovel...
foothills of the famous Black ...
village named 'Egerten'. Becau...
with beautiful hills around, you ca...
everything is simple and excellent...
wine and home-made cakes. It has ...
hundreds of years. The restaurant pe...
way it looks since the last century. Loo...
map north-east from Basel and take the...
there you take a right and drive straight a...
small road ends. There is the 'Gasthaus zu...
Egerten. Call before you like to go from Base...
map and drive about eight miles into the hills ...
(road D 473). Drive straight and you come to a ...
Folgensbourg. A wonderful restaurant named 'Al...
wonderful wine 'Pinot Noir' and wonderful French fa...
The 'Quiche Lorraine' is the best Quiche that I ever a...
'Munster-cheese' is delicious. Every week they serve a ...
main course. Call from Basel for a reservation.
Wolfgang Weingart, Designer, Basel

Gorg

Samar...
... g from ...
..., along ...
... lts and ...
... dday s ...
... Omal...
..., a ta...
... v 7.15...
... cnic, ...
... it at ...
... fores...
... ed A...
... ch, b ...
... table ...
... a/D...

a ...
... eg...
... mp...
... lyn...
... dea...

Amsterdam

Seafood Resta...
Spuistraat 247 ...
Amsterdam witho...
the half of Amster...
popular and relaxi...
Ruedi Rüegg, Desi...

Hotel Pulitzer
Prinsengracht 315-33...
A small, medium price ...
ingeniously created fro...
houses. The style is un...
ards. Lovely quiet inner ...
extensive and knowledge...
Regular, sometimes obsc...
Rodney Fitch, Design Direc...

Valeton & Henstra
Nes 26, 1012 KE Amsterdam ...
Tucked away in a small side s...
Centraal Station, you can trea...
artist's books, and a wide rang...
They also sell current and back...
zegels'. These PTT books on sta...
art Dutch graphics.
Thomas Manss. Designer, London ...

Antiquariaat Schuhmacher
Gelderschekade 107, 1011 EM Ams...
Tel: (020) 6 22 16 04. Fax: (020) 6 2...
Antiquariaat is a bookstore and muse...
architecture, graphic design and art b...
modern 20th century). Original Wendig...
Constructivist items.
James Biber, Architect, New York

Athaneum Bookshop
Spui 14-16
The best selection of magazines and newsp...
the world that I have ever seen, from obscu...
tracts, to the Village Voice, and the Manipula...
to an excellent university bookshop. The Atha...
between the Rokin and the Singel. You can spe...
browsing, before crossing the road for a pils in ...
best of Amsterdam's brown bars, that feels like ...
to be in Suffolk, and you can get a delicious hot ...
wich. Athaneum also has an equally good art boo...
645 Prinsengracht.

Rea...
An or...
stalls ...
Friday a...
Simon S...

Nikos ...
462 A...

Ny...

130

Deyan Sudjic, ...

Paper Nao
1-29-12-201 Sengoku, Bunkyo-ku, Tokyo 112
Tel: (03) 944 4470
Anyone who thinks paper is just paper w...
Naoaki Sakamoto's paper shop. Over...
you can select in a beautifully desig...
of this beige tiled apartment buildi...
Japanese paper. Even if you do...
the paper later, you take me...
them and to feel the surfa...
Hermann Zapf, Designe...

Peponi Hotel
P O Box 24...
The Pepon...
Indian Oc...
designe...
right...
neces...
...

architect's favourite...
contemporary expensive fu...
of course, two large modern...
The view is waterside with old...
people to the archipelago outsi...
master-cook is Bengt Wedholm. ...
...him walk to one of the ships and b...
...ours old.
...strip Sampe, Designer, Stockholm

Wedholms Fish Restaurant (Wedholm...
...fabulous fish restaurant. The fish is the...
...mmercially anywhere. Served impeccab...
...ence of ponceyness. Wedholms is a serio...
...yard, delicious and marvellous restaurant...
...ael Wolff, Designer, London

...kholms Leksakamuseum
...orget 1 C. Tel: (08) 41 61 00
...ly real Toy Museum in the world with toys from...
...e world. Go there, get yourself young again.
...ristiansson, Architect, Stockholm

...undred miles off the coast of Sweden. This...
...he charm of a trip back in time. Especi...
...Garden, small but delightful; Hotel...
...gs converted to a comfortable...
...re. Specialises in wool kni...
...hile still useful. An alt...
...m the usual high...
...a garden. E...
...ee-filled garde...
...July - too man...
...needed; it's too...
...Designer, Connecti...

212

...allenbe...
...ernese...
s Freili...
n Air M...
...from B...
...htful wa...
...ings fro...
...activities...
Open Apri...
...comforta...

...nale Casa...
...a contemp...
...wn has inte...

Le Madri
168 West 18th Stree...
This is the best Italian...
with fine Tuscany food...
duced to me by Marth...
popular, book in advance...
Edward Booth-Clibborn, Pu...

Le Madri
Four old mamas are the chefs a...
Italian recipes with a slightly new...
'in-crowd' also art enthusiasts. Ex...
expensive, reservations required.
Eugene Grossman, Design Consulta...

Bargemusic
Fulton Ferry Landing, Brooklyn, NY 1120...
Every Thursday and Sunday night a cham...
a barge with a huge window overlooking...
district. Musicians of renown from all ov...
in these inspiring concerts. The barge...
Manhattan over the Brooklyn Bridge...
Plaza West (turns to Old Fulton Stre...
and you see it in front of you. (By...
barge is the River Café. Excellent...
Pieter and Annette Brattinga, De...

The Oyster Bar

Yuzu-tei
1-7-11, Nishi-Azabu, Minato-ku. T...
'Yuzu-tei' is a modern Japanese res...
ese style restaurant which make...
serves you the most comfortable...
'Yuzu-tei' serves Japanese food w...
quality and fresh taste of the vege...
will tell you the change of the seas...
seasonal food and by the way of serv...
tableware.
Kenji Ekuan, Designer, Tokyo

Tokyo Bay cruise
Aboard 'Symphony' from Hinode-Samb...
Tel: (03) 453 8100
The most fantastically devel...
front half around the ba...
of 90 or 150 minutes...
panoram...s of a cha...
day...
10.00...
...osts...

41

...ari Christiansson, Architect, ...
...to how many at the...
...in front of chil...

Leopold H...
Near Kär...
According...
Leopold...
founded...
since...
peop...
Jen...

Kappabashi
If you like kitc...
cutting impleme...
been honed to...
camp, in Kappaba...
surrealistic plastic...
real thing and used...
Nick Butler, Designer,...

Joel
Kyodo Building, 2nd Floor...
Minato-ku. Tel: (03) 400 7...
Since the last edition of 'Fe...
upmarket. Still expensive. Sti...
wine, atmosphere and chef are...
dinner - do it.
Ken Cato, Designer, Melbourne

La Taverna...
Via F. Ferruccio...
Great food, grea...
Francois Robert, P...

Scaletta
Piazza Stazione Geno...
Elegant small restau...
of contemporary cera...
Joe Tilson, Artist, Wiltshire

La Brisa
Via Brisa 5. Tel: 87201
An informally elegant restaurant wit...
old trees surrounded by old walls. Y...
there, since all architects and designe...
is light and tasty, the salads are interes...
is always on hand to greet the guests and...
of good wines.
Lella Vignelli, Designer, New York

Locanda del Sant' Uffizio
Cioccaro di Penango, Moncalvo, Asti. Tel: (0141) 9142...
Set in the enchanting hills of Monferrato, the land of w...
varied landscapes, this big aristocratic 17th century man...
house, far from the noise of the town, is perfectly peacef...
surrounded by old trees and with a charming swimming poo...
Reception rooms and bedrooms are beautifully furnished wit...
a good mixture of old and new pieces. The cuisine off...
best of the Piemontese tradition, with absol...
antipasti, splendid pasta and all th...
defend yourself from too...
of course, live u...
Italo Lu...

...G Gakuencho, Higashikurume-shi, Tokyo 202
A lesser known Frank Lloyd Wright building is the...
School. There is an active campaign to save it fr...
Mrs Hani, daughter of the school's founders who...
the building from Wright, is eager to encoura...
come to the site. Contact Hidfya Akagi...
tel: 0424 22 3111.
Sheila Hicks, Artist, Pari...

The Robata...
rest...

pictures are signed W H Yorker and Borstel Temple We...
a delightful discovery to be able to admire Montague...
predecessor in the tiny little fishing resort of the Ligu...
such as Camogli.
Giannetto Coppola, Illustrator, Chiaveri

Il Paradiso
Anyone who has visited the spectacular marble...
Carrara such as Colonnata, knows you have to...
away with the local Grappa... and the best pla...
at Il Paradiso. It's above the village of Querc...
Henraux quarries. They serve fresh trout fro...
where you can also swim and spend a spe...
Michael Lax, Designer, New York

(32km from Piacenza)
A tiny jewel of a medieval hilltown on...
plains. Among other modest attract...
with good food, views.
La Rocca-da Franco tel (0523) 80...
La Taverna del Falconiere tel (05...
Helen & Gene Federico, Designe...

Hotel Salivolpi
53011 Castellina in Chianti...
Tel: (0577) 740484. Fax:...
This very sensitive and cl...
Tuscan farmhouse retai...
not have a restaurant....
snacks by the pool wi...
Gimignano or bring in...
restaurants and vine...
equidistant from Si...
We met journalists...
had spent many h...
countryside, foo...
Jessica Strang...

Osteria co...
Via Bighet...
A typical...
Genoa,...
restaur...
cookin...
fish,...
well...
Eu...

...overlooking w...
50 mussels cooked in o...
other fish dishes - and a bott...
very modest cost.
Herbert Spencer, Designer, Lo...

Victor Horta House
Amerikastraat 23-25, Sint Gilles...
Open: Tuesday - Sunday, 14.00...
When you are in Brussels and hav...
house, do go. Victor Horta (186...
nouveau architect, who designed...
beautiful buildings in Brussels, bu...
1898, when he was at the peak o...
house, actually a double house fo...
today a museum, perfect and undam...
most complete, perfect and undan...
nouveau architecture.
Wim Crouwel, Designer, Rotterdam

La Méditerranée Tel: 512 73 08
...des Chartreux. Tel: 512 73 08
moules et frites in Bru...

La Grillade au Feu de Bois. Tel: 94 69 71 20
Flassans-sur-Issole.
Coming from Aix-en-Provence and following the N7 direction
Nice, you'll find at 4 km before arriving in Le Luc on your left-
hand this lovely 18th century farmhouse, where you can stay
the night or just have an excellent 'Provence' meal on a lovely
terrace under a 200 year old mulberry tree. And please taste
the nicest wine in this region: the 'Bernarde'. In Le Luc-en-
Provence itself you find the interesting National Stamp Mu...
Dick Bruna, Illustrator, Utrecht.

Au chat qui pêche
17 rue des débris Saint Etienne, 598...
Tel: (20) 51 87 42
Most English tourists bypass L...
plates are so uncommon th...
into, as ours was within...
fascinating city, with...
17th century stoc...
flowers, masks...
they no long...
served b...
front...
...

Many designers

    find it extremely difficult

    to produce

    unless they are working

    to severe deadlines.

I'm not one of them.

    To my thinking that means one

    lacks the opportunity

    to savour the sensual pleasure

    of doing it.

I find deadlines

    similar to the condition

    induced by a brand of beer

    in the Cameroons.

Here one passes directly

    from sobriety to hangover,

    without an intervening

    stage of drunkenness.

AF

The work in this section explores the relationship between writing, drawing and meaning – a form of communication which can express anything from city buildings to a complex emotion or an intellectual idea.

'The trick,' according to Fletcher, 'is to bring the visual proposition up to the edge so that you have both a letter and an abstract sign. Two things instead of one.' In transcribing the Hong Kong or Manhattan skyline, he actually ends up with three things – the letters, the form, and the name itself.

He is selective with the tools he uses in making these letter drawings. The kind of ink can affect the shape of letter, different papers can cause different qualities of line. 'A Staedtler Lumographic E pencil has great intensity, which is just right for some jobs.' But not apparently for others. 'If it looks a scribble,' he says, 'then at least it's a thoughtful scribble.'

The title for a French book jacket on art (below) was carefully squeezed out in acrylics directly from the tubes. The client said it looked like icing on a cake and rejected it. In both cases he was probably right.

Penmanship can be used to complement or contradict a notion. Note how the tall serif-capital grandeur of the word 'Criticism' is sharply cancelled by an angrily scrawled 'Against'.

The 'Best of British Authors' makes a more whimsical interpretation, as writing becomes drawing becomes caricature. This image is from a poster commissioned by the Book Marketing Council to promote Britain's greatest living writers. In the taxi cab on the way back to his studio from the briefing, he began to doodle. The core of the idea came to him almost immediately. The thought of a great writer evoked an image of the bust of an honourable man. So he drew a bust which turns into a pen nib and writes what the promotion is all about. Not only does this reveal his capacity to treat an initial doodle as a finished design, it also shows his facility to turn inanimate objects into animate figures.

The forceful page of writing on the right says what it says. Here is a double plagiarism: the coffee stain from an espresso cup is an idea borrowed from a letterhead done by designer Bob Gill for his wife many years previously; the expressive writing is an oblique homage to Saul Steinberg. 'I'm sure Bob won't mind,' says Alan, ' but I'm not so sure about Steinberg.'

I rewrite like anything and ~~more~~ chopping and pruning & mucking about until I like the sound of it — its _important TO SEE how it looks._

(Patrick Leigh Fermor)

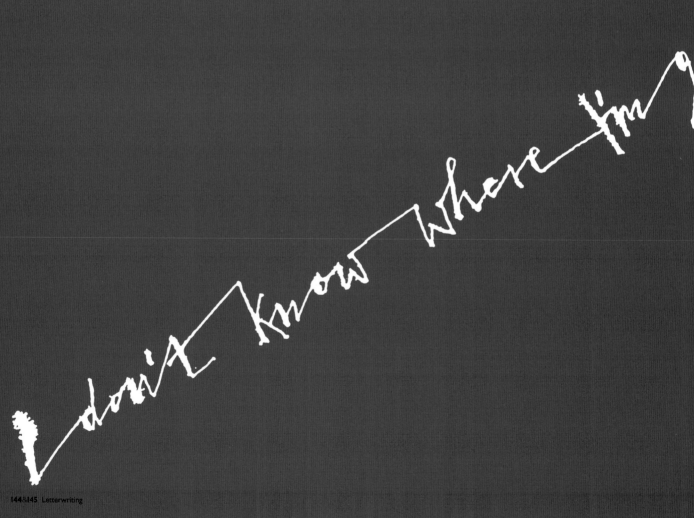

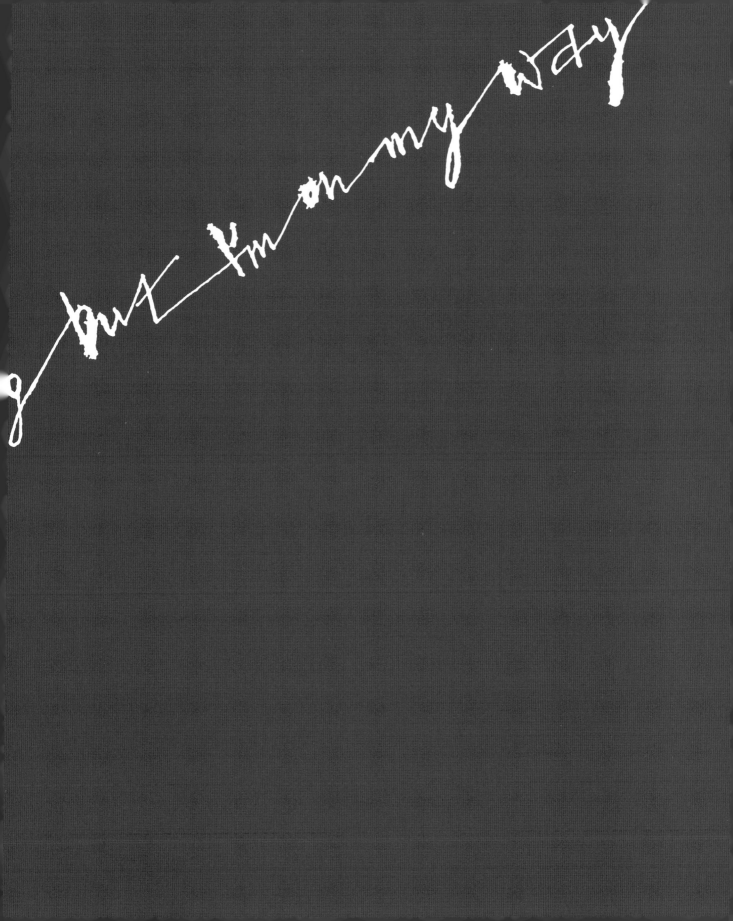
but I'm on my way

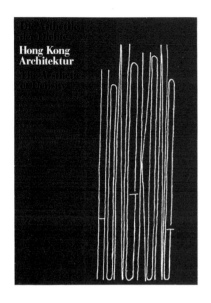

These designs, which relate the names of places to their built form, were all completed within a two-year period, another example of a fondness for returning to the same notion once it has taken hold in his mind.

The silver on Chinese-red skyline of Hong Kong was a poster for the Deutsches Architektur Museum in Frankfurt. The density of letters was intended to reflect the title and subject of the exhibition. The configuration of Stonehenge, again drawn to represent rather than imitate, was for a book jacket on the monument's future. By using non-waterproof ink, the splodge of yellow diffused the lettering to create the solstice, and the dazzle of seeing the stones against the sun.

The drawing of Manhattan was a contribution to a promotional exercise launched by designer Massimo Vignelli to persuade the city to erect a sculpture – a Big Apple. Vignelli asked design colleagues around the world to send in their interpretation of Manhattan. Here is Fletcher's.

Overleaf

The calligraphic image of *Amore* (love) celebrated a friend's marriage in Rome, and shows that design, like marriage itself, can often be a matter of equilibrium. Whilst in the calligraphic image which faces it, the words themselves answer their own question.

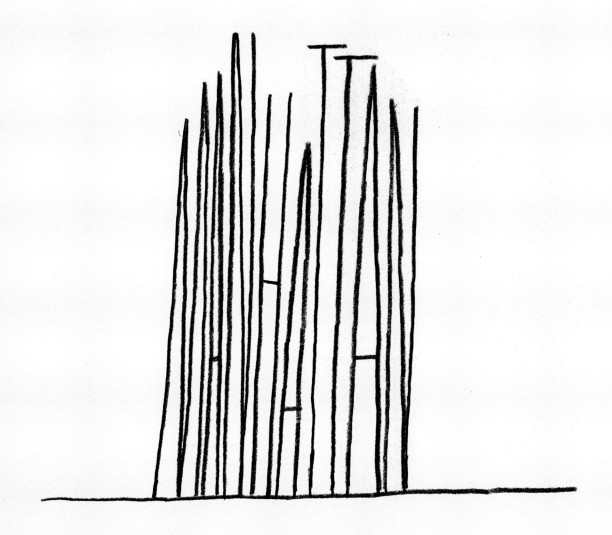

View driving in from
the Triboro bridge

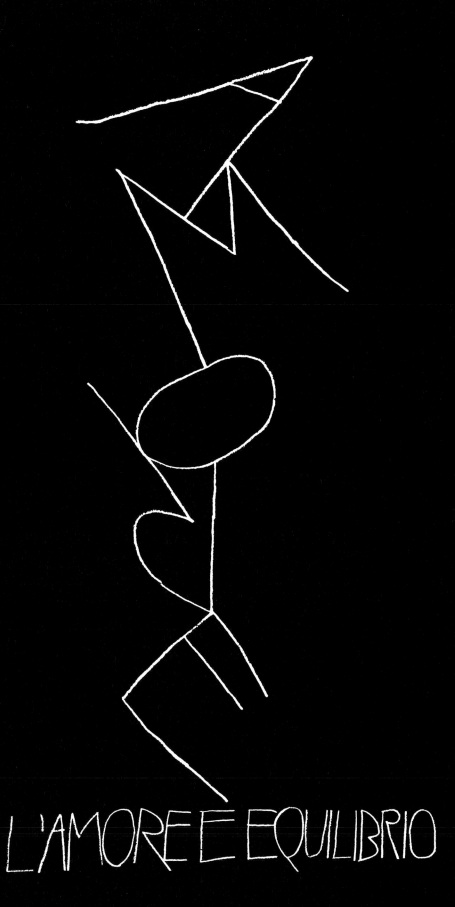

L'AMORE E EQUILIBRIO

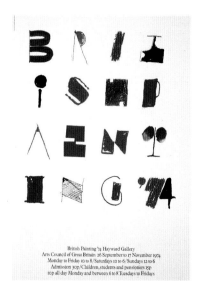

British Painting '74 Hayward Gallery
Arts Council of Great Britain 26 September to 17 November 1974
Monday to Friday 10 to 8/Saturdays 10 to 6/Sundays 12 to 6
Admission 30p/Children, students and pensioners 15p
10p all day Monday and between 6 to 8 Tuesdays to Fridays

The Art Book draws on the extraordinarily rich archives of art and design publisher Phaidon. It presents an A to Z of famous artists as an accessible introduction to the world of fine art. For instance, Leonardo Da Vinci and Roy Lichtenstein share a spread. Each letter on the cover (shown opposite), employs a different technique, medium or texture – to express the variety of painting styles demonstrated within.

As well as having many connections with his other work, *The Art Book* cover revisits a design of more than twenty years ago, when Fletcher first began to explore solutions rooted in the alphabet and take them beyond the boundaries of conventional typography. A poster for the Arts Council combined the subject and title of the exhibition by treating each letter as a miniature painting. Exercises fusing expression with content.

Overleaf

This title for a design seminar uses a different instrument to draw each letter – crayon, thin Rapidograph, the wrong end of a brush in ink, ballpoint, cut paper, and a soft (and smudged) pencil. Together they spell an appropriate word.

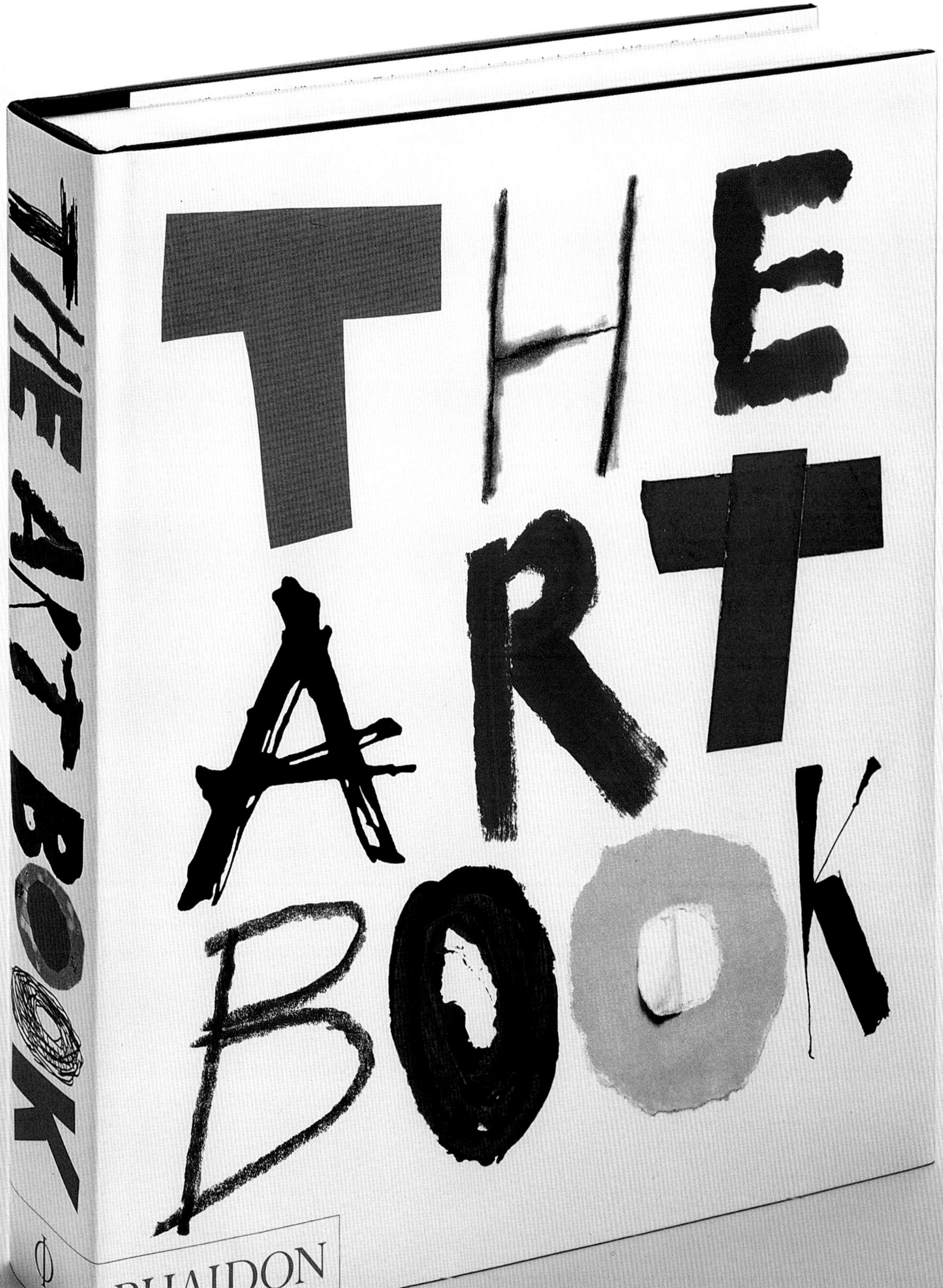

THE ART BOOK

PHAIDON

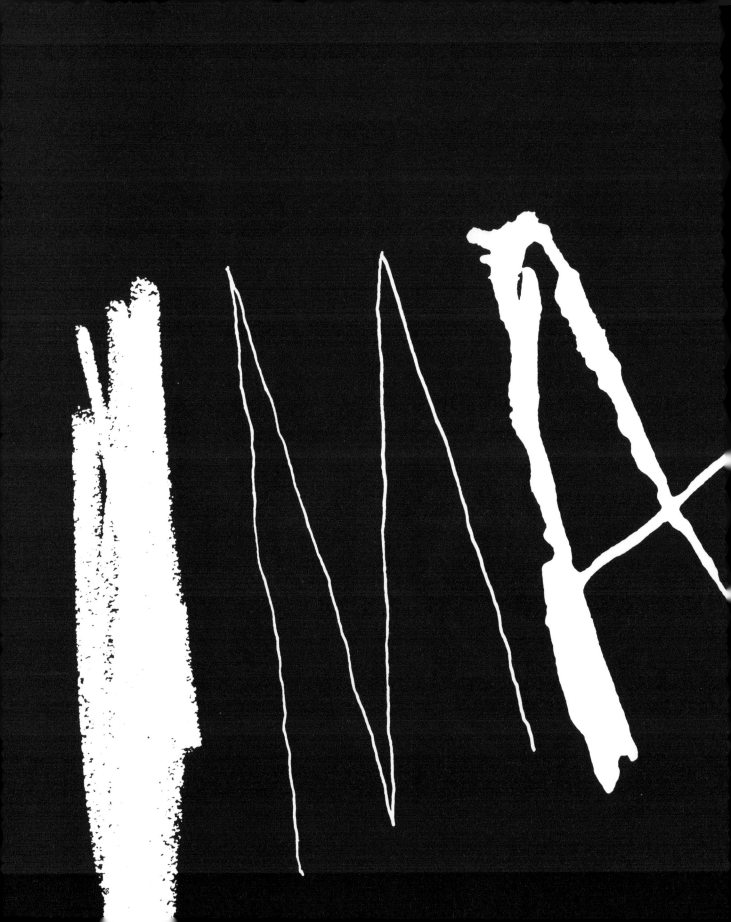

Whereas painters are concerned with solving their own problems,

designers occupy themselves solving other people's problems.

Actually that's an oversimplification.

Their aim goes beyond finding a solution;

it's the elegance of the solution that counts.

That's a personal challenge rather than utilitarian discipline.

A commitment rather than an involvement.

A difference exampled by a plate of ham and eggs.

Here the pig is committed –

whereas the chicken is merely involved.

AF

The design of signs for buildings that are architectural landmarks, or are complex in their functional layout, or both, represent some of the most difficult challenges a graphic designer is likely to face. This section looks briefly at four of Alan Fletcher's sign programmes: for Richard Roger's Lloyd's of London building in the city, for Norman Foster's Stansted Airport Terminal, for the Victoria & Albert Museum, and for the IBM European headquarters at Tour Pascal in Paris. All of these projects required a diverse approach as they all presented different problems.

These projects reflect his belief that signs, in addition to their purpose, should be tailored to the environment in which they appear. The last thing that architects who create exciting and innovative buildings want are signs that will detract from the aesthetic clarity of their work or awkwardly impose their presence – signs should complement and enhance their surroundings.

The S gn Company

But such are the complexities inherent in wayfinding that paradoxically many schemes lose their way, mainly because of the vested interests one has to accommodate. Satisfying the architect is one thing but having to cope with the often contradictory demands of other factions in the client mix can rapidly erode any clear concept. Added to these difficulties are the technical problems of specification, materials, schedules, manufacture and installation, ensuring you are in for a long hard ride. 'Doing a programme for a public space like an airport is like trench warfare,' he observes. 'You're fighting to hold onto a position but you know that you will eventually have to retreat.'

(Logotype for a sign manufacturer)

Lloyd's of London building

The governing idea for the concrete and steel-clad expanses of Lloyd's was to use a stencil (attributed to Le Corbusier) to frame the information so that one could look directly through the signs to read the architecture. Right-angling the sign panels enabled them to be inserted between the joints of the steel cladding, which was already in place on site, and to project out from the walls, thus increasing visibility. Signs encircling columns were spaced off the surface and other fixing variations were developed to ensure sensitive integration with the interiors. Colour coding was used to identify the various levels and areas. The assignment reveals Fletcher's ability to reduce a problem to its bare essentials, and yet also come up with an aesthetic, innovative and appropriate answer.

Likewise, a planning requirement to install something which would impede a runaway truck careering down Leadenhall Street and crashing into the building, produced a positive response. The maritime roots of the Lloyd's insurance business prompted the solution; a large cylindrical granite drum with a compass rose (properly aligned) was inlaid in the top surface. This is now a local landmark and encourages people to sit on it at lunchtime while having their sandwiches.

Some of the most intelligent people in the world can get totally lost in the Victoria & Albert Museum. This rambling nineteenth-century building is uniquely disorienting as one vast space simply opens into yet another. There is a central garden courtyard but you can't easily locate it because of the blinds which shield the artifacts from sunlight. As a consequence, visitors rarely know where they are, or on which floor they are standing, or even in which direction they face. Finding a method to guide them around was further complicated by the need to avoid interfering with the ornate ceilings and decorated walls found in many of the spaces. These are priceless artifacts in their own right. Such were the constraints.

After analyzing the situation, Fletcher concluded that installing directional signs would turn the V&A into a museum of signs. However, if people couldn't be directed, they should at least know where they were located. The answer was to introduce an orientation system based on a colour-coded compass indicating north, east, west and south. The relevant directional colour was repeated on the signs, and a colour-coded floor plan of the exhibits given to visitors when they entered the museum. For instance if a visitor looked north, they would see signs in the representative

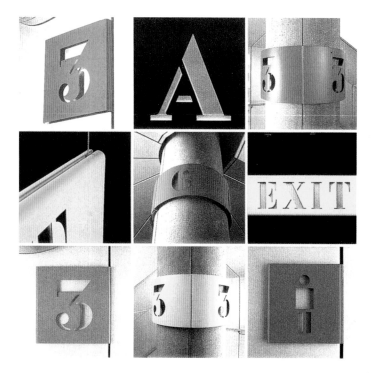

CHINA
Export Art

CHINA
3000 BC to the present

INDIA
ISLAM
EXIT

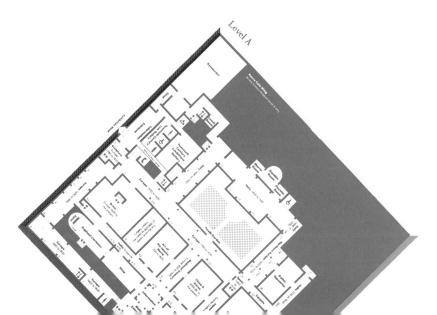

Level A

The Victoria & Albert Museum

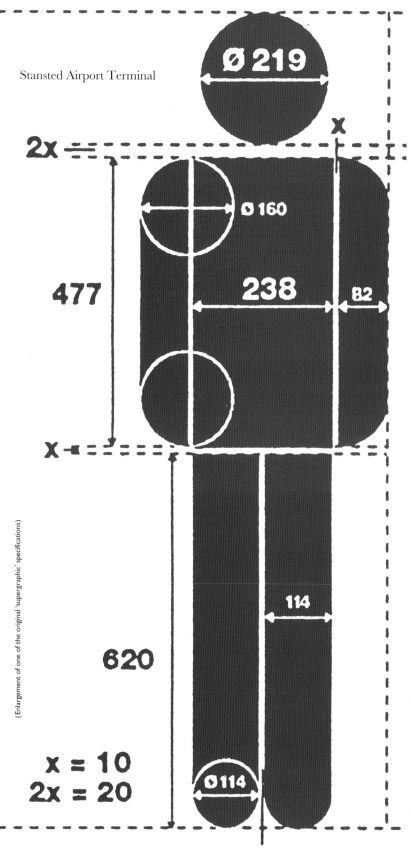

Stansted Airport Terminal

Ø 219

2x

Ø 160

477

238

82

X

X

114

620

x = 10
2x = 20

Ø114

X

(Enlargement of one of the original 'supergraphic' specifications)

colour, and by orienting the plan they would know which way they wanted to go. Additional guidance was to be provided by displaying enlarged plans and small scale models of the building at salient points.

All of that seemed feasible but there still remained the intractable problem of how to clearly signal the spaces and identify the permanent collections. It was the recollection of seeing old military flags hanging in Westminster Abbey that suggested the thought of using banners. An additional idea was to reproduce the information in different classical typefaces, so that each banner would in itself contribute to the V&A collection. Unfortunately this proved too costly and the compromise was to use letters originally designed by Giambattista Bodoni in the eighteenth century.

The scheme began to unravel almost as soon as it was unveiled. The programme could only be partially implemented due to severe funding shortfalls and so it proceeded piecemeal and eventually ground to a halt. Banners were not properly lit, some were hung in the dark, some still are. The floor plan handed out to visitors was reissued without the compass colours (yet another cost saving) which made a complete nonsense of the colour scheme. Today the V&A still remains all but impossible to negotiate. In fact it's got much worse. Subsequent additions have infested the museum with a clutter of non-compatible signs.

Architect Norman Foster had seen the Lloyd's scheme and asked Fletcher to do the sign system for Stansted Airport. A structure conceived as an open, light and transparent building, which required minimal signs because the procedures were self-evident: as the passengers entered the terminal, they could see right through to the planes. At least that was the premise, but it isn't just old buildings that elude innovative and effective routing solutions.

The first task was to work out exactly which signs were necessary, where they should be located, what size they should be, and how they could be displayed. This was done by marking passenger routes and fixing sight lines on detailed architectural plans of the areas.

The design concept was based on using 'supergraphics' and giant sculptures of arrows, letters and symbols (see left) so facilities could be identified from a distance. The intention being to reduce the number of directional signs to a minimum and so avoid the visual noise and clutter associated with most terminals.

However, the airport authority rejected the proposals insisting that their corporate sign manual should be strictly followed, despite the fact that the structure and interior space was radically different from their other air terminals. For example, it contained no intervening walls or ceilings from which to hang signs.

This compromise became increasingly complicated as the design also had to satisfy the often conflicting wishes of a burgeoning multiplicity of clients – the architects, the airport authorities, the airlines, flight information, fire officers, customs, security staff, baggage handling companies, passport controls and quite a few others. The process was further compounded by the rapidly decreasing budgets and the increasing pressures to meet schedules. Once into the programme there was little choice (or time) to do more than try to preserve as much of the original concept as was possible. As Foster once remarked about architecture: design is often reduced to politics.

A greater measure of success in implementation was achieved when IBM Europe commissioned the signs for their headquarters in Tour Pascal, two new office towers in Paris. These were named after Blaise Pascal, whose mechanical calculating machine prefigured the modern computer.

In this case the nature of the project imposed different challenges. IBM has a well-controlled and established corporate identity and the signs had to conform to style. There was also a physical problem in that the two separate towers were only connected on the ground and lower levels, and via a bridge on the nineteenth floor. A situation that required elaborate directions to guide people around. Finally the 2,000 staff underwent a 40 percent annual turnover as headquarter's policy was to recruit secondees from national companies for short periods. This meant information and nameplate directories had to be easily interchangeable.

Finances dictated adapting a commercially available panel system rather than creating a bespoke solution. The design process therefore became one of juggling with predetermined elements: the corporate typefaces, standard panel units and the constantly changing identification of names for the offices.

Corporate organizations such as IBM have the kind of programmatic administrative structure and purpose which lends itself to consistent if somewhat predictable solutions. But whether in public spaces or commercial buildings, designing a method of wayfinding that is both effective, aesthetic and imaginative, appears to remain the Holy Grail.

IBM Europe headquarters

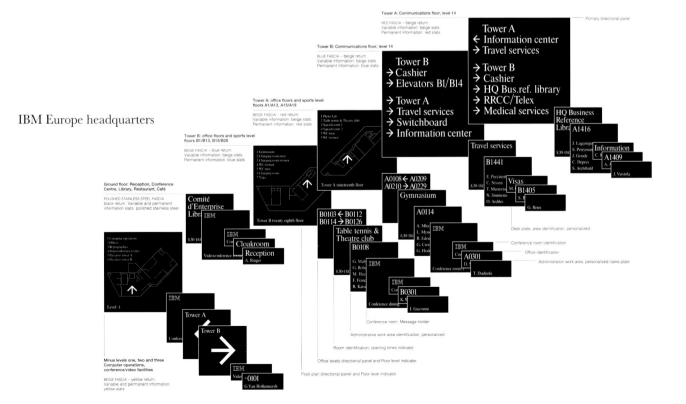

A greeting card

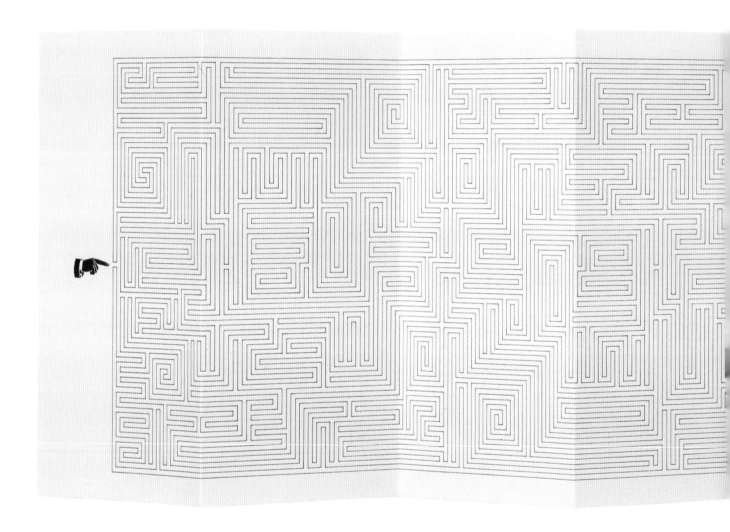

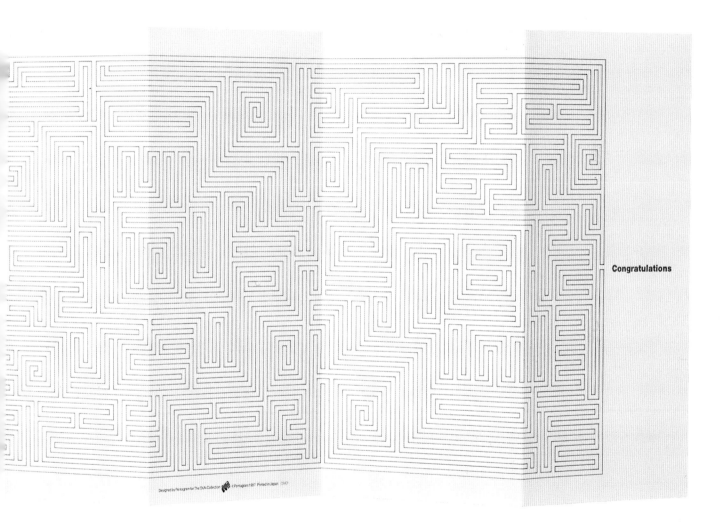

Congratulations

Designed by Pentagram for The DUN Collection © Pentagram 1987 Printed in Japan

The Banyan Tree

Most of us remember someone who opened a door in our minds.
'Why are you drawing the tree like that?' queried the
art teacher. I said I didn't know but that was how I felt
like doing it. He asked why I felt like doing it like that.
I confessed I didn't know. 'You should', he said, 'otherwise
how can you really draw the tree?' I still didn't understand.
Eventually I did. Of course there are also those who close
doors. Making a colour composition another teacher once
sharply admonished me saying, 'We never use orange!' She
was a formidable lady and I didn't dare ask why — even now
I look over my shoulder if I use orange. I was also taught by
Josef Albers (painter and colourist) who believed teaching was
a matter of asking the right questions rather than giving
the right answers. Not that he was exactly open minded. He
used to say Matisse didn't know anything about colour and
regularly picked me out in class with his cold eye to state
that the English had no taste. But by then I'd learnt what,
and what not, to listen to. If your mind is too open people can
throw all sorts of rubbish into it.

(The Banyan Tree, Ficus Virens, was the Tree of Knowledge under which Buddha gained enlightenment. Walked...

Alan Fletcher is alive to the potential of some of the most incongruous of objects. The designs in these pages deftly recycle miscellaneous bits and pieces he has picked up in the street, which have caught his eye in a market, or which just happened to be around his studio.

'Ready-mades', as they are called, can acquire entirely new meanings depending on the context in which they are placed, or how they are used. They might be playing cards or old photographs or postage stamps. Sometimes connections are made by uniting opposed elements. One such memorable image is an Eames chair upholstered in floral fabrics. Another example, a sketch on a serviette, summons up a bold response to the question of how to redesign the charred hall at Windsor Castle. Whatever is being recycled, Alan Fletcher will put it to work.

These are two cover designs for the Italian magazine *Domus*. The issue which is published during the same month as the annual Milan Furniture Fair is especially important and to take a classic Eames chair, that icon of Modernism, and cover it with floral fabrics not only reflects the sense of creative outrage with which some exhibitors have always sought to associate themselves, but is also an ironical comment on taste in general. It was accompanied by the caption: *De Gustibus non est disputandum.* Incidentally the man painting Fletcher's studio at the time said he thought it looked lovely, and asked to borrow a copy to take home so he could do up his sofa.

The incongruous marriage of a bird target from a French shooting gallery with a statue of a British general was produced to demonstrate the hazards of urban planning. The combination of words and picture invests the image with an additional charge.

images

For information please contact:
Banks Sadler Ltd, 15 Pratt Mews
London NW1 0AD, Tel (071) 388 9101
Telex 261200, Fax (071) 383 4794

Wolfgang Weingart (Swi) on typography
Peter Brookes (UK) on illustration
Henry Steiner (Hong Kong) on symbols
Martin Pedersen (USA) on magazines

Theme of the seminar:
The design process
from the idea to
the final solution

Seventeenth Icograda Student Seminar
9:30am to 12:00 on 11/12 February 1991
Odeon Cinema, Marble Arch, London
International Council of Graphic Design Associations

When wondering over breakfast what to give his friend Fergus Henderson as a present for his wedding, the post arrived. Now for most people an envelope is no more than an envelope, but in Alan Fletcher's eyes it may be more significant than the letter inside. The mail, by coincidence, had one envelope with these two postage stamps illustrating Carrickfergus Castle. An additional piece of luck was that they were superimposed by two circular franking marks. As Fergie sports big round glasses, the only missing ingredient to be added was his characteristic broad smile. The resulting portrait was the wedding present.

This poster (left) combines three recurring themes – ready-made objects, playing with type, and making faces. The two old Kodak slide mounts, forming the eyes, were turned upside-down so that the familiar swish of the logo could generate eyelashes. The features were banged out on an old Olivetti Lettra 22 typewriter, a choice of means which closely follows the 'found object' principle, and the black background was selected to put the audience in the dark.

Common objects can represent alternative ideas. Fletcher found an old cinema ticket, saw the connection between hole and letter, stuck it down on a piece of board and sent it to his good friend Bob as a Christmas card. The two razorblade packs (left) were discovered on a market stall in southern Italy. Both Bob Geers and Bob Gross (neither of them the Bob referred to above), were the owners of an advertising agency. They used to play tricks on their clients by each pretending to be the other over the phone, as they both sounded exactly the same. Hence the thought behind the picture, which finally ended up hanging on the wall of their executive toilet. Another connection was made by selecting and arranging two playing cards, the nine being a mirror image of the six, into an original Valentine – albeit with a risqué twist.

Even a standard label can make an ironical comment, in this case on a talking shop for designers. The poster promoted the 1993 Design Renaissance Congress in Glasgow. Fletcher noticed the label on a discarded carton which was lying upside-down, an incongruous position given the message it carried. He considered that a seminar such as the Design Renaissance would give people an excuse to air dogmatic views, so that became his theme. He simply stuck down the ready-made label on a scrap of paper, jotted down the slogan and sent it to the printer, circumventing the process of design and specification. The details of the congress are set down the side in miniscule type. Seeing the potential in the ordinary requires a perceptive mind as well as a discerning eye.

Squashing space can reveal
hidden environments —
like the support of this small palm

THIS WAY UP

DOWN WITH DOGMA

Items of Kykeana

Here is a creative, offbeat, improvised solution to
the complex challenge of what to do with the charred
remains of the fire-damaged historic St George's Hall
at Windsor Castle. During 1993 the Architecture
Foundation decided to invite twelve British designers
and architects to exhibit their suggestions. Fletcher
sketched his on a serviette and sent that in, together
with this explanation:

*The debate revolves around whether to reconstruct or redesign.
My inclination is to do neither, but to leave the gutted and charred
remains exactly as they are. My proposal is to throw a glass
canopy over the exposed roof, insert a freestanding, narrow steel
deck on stilts down the centre of the aisle mounted from each end
by an elegant lightweight staircase of steel and glass. Hanging
from the roof and slung beneath the deck are projectors (film / video /
slide) to throw images on the different areas and surfaces of the
ruined interior. These would visually recreate the various styles
the Hall has undergone in the past: Gothic, Baroque, Victorian
– the conflagration itself – and the new architectural proposals.
The constantly changing scenes would create an everchanging
theatrical backdrop for the functions taking place on the deck:
ceremonial affairs, Garter lunches, state banquets, masked balls.*

NOTE: *In 1999 a supper was held in St George's Hall by the
Architecture Foundation finally to resolve the debate. During
the supper I did a sketch on my serviette of the scene around
me from my dining table on the steel deck.*

A Greek coffee drawn in Greek coffee

Overleaf

Whenever Alan Fletcher is dining with fellow designers,
wherever he is, he invariably asks them to draw on
a serviette as a memento. They can do whatever they
like – a doodle, a sketch, a self-portrait, a comment,
anything. Over the years he has amassed a formidable
collection of serviettes by the famous, the talented and
the famously talented.

The doodles are revealing about their authors. Some
of his distinguished friends are inhibited about drawing
in front of their peers. They procrastinate. They fiddle.
André François said flatly: 'I can't draw in public' and
wrote that down on the serviette. Kurt Weideman took
the serviette home and sent it back three months later
– a Robert Frost poem decorated with buttons. In a
French village, Seymour Chwast just gazed out of the
restaurant window across a village square and drew
the scene before him. In Manhattan Milton Glaser
dipped the end of a fork in red wine and did a portrait.
In a restaurant in Bologna Roman Cieslewicz asked
the waiter for a pair of scissors and cut out eyes, nose
and Fletcher's distinctive scar. While Massimo Vignelli,
passing the time with Fletcher in a Tokyo drinking
club, drew a series of naked Geisha girls labelled with
the Japanese names for the parts of the body. The
Geishas giggled uncontrollably at such very personal
questions and his struggle with the spelling. 'It's not
so much the drawings,' he says, 'but what they reveal
about the people who did them.'

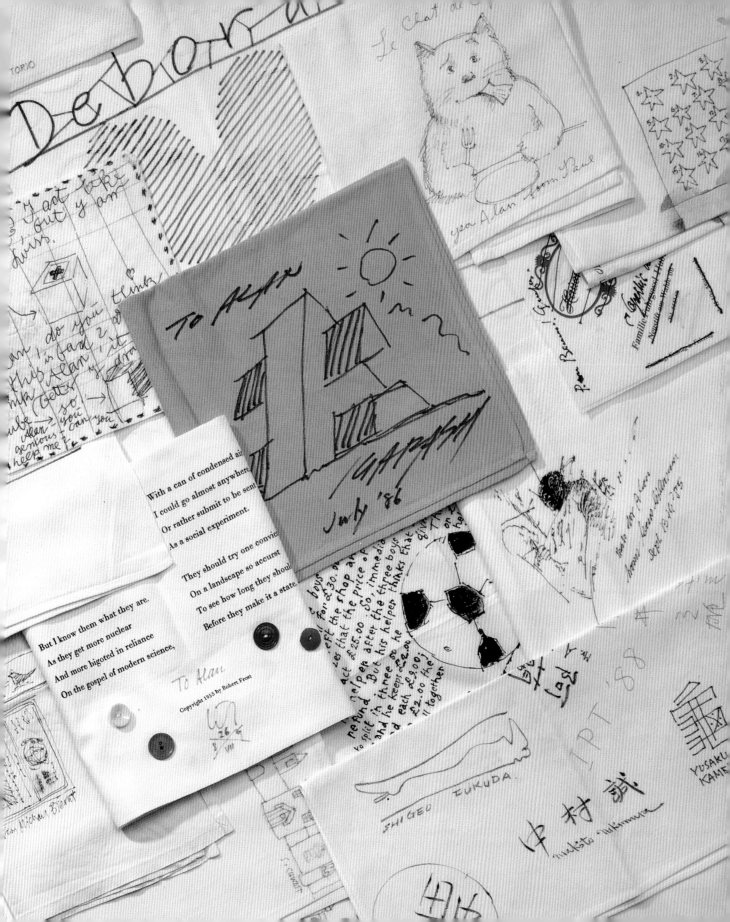

All along the hot streets of Gaudi's city are unpainted buildings in which dark men and women work at their lives without ever asking the question why. In their midst, but still outside, stands a young stranger. He has finished with his first art school. His real education is just beginning. He looks around. What he sees is not what those men and women see. He sees the art of living and marks of history in the walls, the doors, the signs and inscriptions, the water in the fountain, the taberna in the corner, the campanario above. Now he wants to be what he sees; be the art of living, be a mark of history. So he draws back the Victorian net curtains and lets in the light. The Fifties had started. There may have been a war; there may have been an empire, but they are not going to get him now. He ceases to care whether anyone is with him. He knows he can see. There may be others, but he does not yet know who they are. Armed with a talent that will prevent him becoming an 'artist', he starts trying to live.

Later, about twenty years later, with people beginning to applaud him when he walks into a room, he really does wonder if this is what he meant to do. He works by the window in a star London studio. There is no street outside, just the cool and empty calm of the Grand Union canal below. The studio stretches into the distance. Others had come along. They were all celebrities now. There had already been so many kind words, so many admiring glances and questions. There had also been stiletto jabs, both critical and jealous. And of course there had been men with money, prepared to pay. There had been all the seductions and complications of business success that destroy simplicity. It was really time to leave, but he stayed and prospered and became older.

After another twenty years, he is here in his own whitewashed studio. He did leave in the end. The pleasures and the conflicts that he discovered in the heat of the streets all those years ago continue to absorb him. Much more than the architect, who designs for life, most of his work is life - enjoyment, movement, smiles, poignancy, some sadness and, of course, light. He has learned much, but somehow he doesn't let it show. Unencumbered by the accumulations of his life, he has, curiously, given up or thrown away very little. In his client list,

'Every act of rebelling expresses a nostalgia for innocence and an appeal to the essence of being.' Albert Camus, THE REBEL, 1951

short but senior, is a magazine from Milan. And there in her house, only a huge sliding door away, is the girl from Bologna whom he met strawberry picking in the Fens forty years earlier. And there on a stool is their girl talking Italian on the phone to the accounts department in Milan. This scene is at odds with his reputation for hard-headed worldliness, not how they said it would be. But this is the same man with the same way of getting things done. What he has achieved is not harmony, but equilibrium. A matter of balance between making and taking; balance between work, pleasure and the responsibility of making the money that feeds both. He has achieved the organization that suits him through pragmatism as well as by design. His books are not arranged by author or subject, but by size. For a man so committed to wet inks, soft pencils and papers, he nevertheless also uses the disdained brittle light of the electronic screen because it helps him produce and organize. (The qualities of touch and texture do not subsume electronic graphics.) So he sits down at a huge white desk. A very large, round glass ashtray catches most of the grey dandruff from his millionth cigarette. He is working.

Now he has been asked to do a new job. He sets his mind once more against the sins of laziness and convention, and starts to look around for ideas. First there are magpie thoughts, collecting through the archives of his mind. These archives are the place he has built in which to dwell and think and dabble and explore, constructed while looking and seeing, teaching, reading, working and playing. The place is full of references: large spaces and lofts, tiny crevices and corners, surprising recesses. It has foundations of rubble, discarded lumps of formal upbringing and education, through which run precious veins of enlightenment and learning. The floors are his friends, fellows and peers who are his measure. He walks around them, over them, on them. The walls are experience, identity and self-esteem, sober and not grafted or contrived. The windows let in the light, and remind him that there are always contexts and connections; there is no isolation. If anyone tries to peer in, he usually pulls down the blinds. And then there are the steps and staircases. Up he goes looking around, getting stuck, going down again, starting up again. The ceilings are images and colours, words, shapes and textures that are the elements used to execute ideas, not only his own but those of others all over the world. Above them is the roof, which is not finished. He can still see the sky.

For all its resources, this place is not self-contained. He often has to leave it to go and talk to people to help him find the idea that will start the job. He will ask and argue, reason and exasperate. Anti-democratic by nature, he is nevertheless deferential to those with ideas of their own. But he is wary of the ability of discussion and consensus to change and destroy. He would want everyone to agree and see it the way he does, and if they don't it often makes no difference. He can often get other people to do and think what he wants them to - by appeals to their vanity and by conjuring up visions of importance for them. And he can be hard on those around him, especially the flabby or sycophantic, but even harder on himself; yet also patient with himself, as impatient with others. For underlying these processes is a single-minded struggle for insight, for meaning in concepts. Each job he regards as being a test of his beliefs. He has not foregone the excitement of discovery that shrivels up in so many as they replace their creative endeavours with the running of ever more complicated lives. He is still on his own road of intellectual freedom; the man who looks around to see the problem from the other side.

Like the problem, his solution will contain challenges. At some point it occurred to him, either because he had been told so or because it was admirable, that the idea of all graphic design was to find within the brief a visual answer that contained its own set of questions and answers; a crossword clue set as an answer not a question. In there is an answer - there may be more than one. This is the game. These are the rules. It's vastly entertaining, especially for him - I've worked out how to do this job, now you can work out why it's right. Looking as he does for new ways of playing his game, the results - selected, tested, layered and larded - are still often knowingly referential. Thus in his work you may detect the stern enlightenment of Kandinsky being played off against the best jester antics of Klee (the nod and the wink), the hilarious shock tactics of the Dadaist, the unity of type, shapes, colours and materials espoused by the central European Constructivist and the Dutch De Stijl, the Expressionist's flight from inhibition, even the Italian Futurist's eye for words combined with graphic form. Despite a formative sojourn in and around Madison Avenue, which taught him what money can do and how to break rules constructively, his style is discernibly European.

But for all its influences and riches, the twentieth-century graphic revolutions have not imprisoned him. Such is the intellectual grasp of his craft that he can justly claim that it has an ancestry as old as the inscriptions on Trajan's column or even the Egyptian hieroglyphs and Middle Eastern scripts from five thousand years ago. Add to all this background the thousands of visual incidents and accidents that have caught his educated and agile eye in the world around him - the trivial catches of light and passing connections and compositions that can spell out meaning - and he has the material to weave into interpretation and compound into a new graphic. As well as the quality of light, form and line, he is caught by atmosphere, derived from the presence of people who may not inhabit the composition, but are implied nevertheless. The observer still on the outside, but with such a sense of life.

Even though he relishes the brightness, colour and the heat of places further south, this man is English. He has English irony, not French; English composure, not German; English mischief, not Italian; English loyalty, not American. He retains much of the insularity he was born with and into, and he has an English lack of regard for the English stereotype. This is the tension that, both through work and choice, has driven him to practically every part of the world pursuing the cosmopolitan in a way that seems obsessive, but has as much to do with the opportunities his reputation has provided as with any scheme. To be more particular, his England is London, where he works and lives. It is London that resonates to those notes and harmonies he understands best. In his own way he helped create them, along with the laughing band of artists, designers and photographers that made up the avant garde of the 1950s and 1960s. That was a time. When all those experiments and expressions in ideas, techniques and materials produced such exciting and seductive imagery. Art had often been used in words before, but as the ghost of Futurism breathed on Pop, words used in art as art especially appealed to him. The idea that ideas can be expressed using words whilst remaining graphic was also the basis of the marriage between typographer and art director that had been the glory of New York years earlier. He had been there too. Thus the typographical illustration and illustrative typography became the mainstay of the new graphic design of which he became one of the most fêted protagonists. Eventually the formalism inherent in typography began to frighten him so he

countered it more and more, first by increasing the juggling and colouring of letterforms, then by giving himself an even freer hand with the frequent use of the pencil and pen. This was through no disrespect to the typographic arts, with which he has great affinity, but to ensure that they did not become a constraint to his thinking or a limitation to his scope.

Two things have been necessary to keep his complex engine of knowledge, experience and concentration well oiled and fully serviced: money and a kind of self-indulgence. Money is required to act both as a measure of respect and as a servant of work. Having been in partnership for thirty years with others who had together produced a reputation that outshone any in the world, he could demand and command very large sums for his creations. This was never simple greed. Money was required to keep the edifice of the reputation in order and thus the work flowing. He also needed enough for himself so he would not have to waste his time going down to the launderette. Money could build bank accounts and make other people rich; or it could keep opening up new places for him to look around. So he asked for it, often more of it than was originally offered in order to do a better job than was expected. Does it meet the brief and budget? is not the way he likes to test his work. A job is not a meal ticket but an opportunity to develop and build. It goes like this. First presentation: This is what you asked me to do, but while I was about it I came up with another approach. If you spent a little more it would be better, don't you think? Yes. Next meeting: I've had this thought - if you're going to do it the way we agreed, why don't you take the opportunity to do this too - make the most of your investment? Okay... . And so the job builds and more money is spent, because the quality of the improvements is unquestionable. This is done without guile, despite some jeering from those who have observed the process. It may mean that the original budget is busted, but then what is produced is more and better, and everyone benefits.

Close to the end of the day he moves easily into a kind of self-indulgence which is his hedonistic counterpoint to the monk-like devotion required by his daytime work. This is not a time when he forgets what he is doing; it is just another facet of his all-consuming occupation. This is a time to be more expansive, to forsake the inner archives. His sociability is hardly voluble and never verbose, at once enthusiastic and taciturn and usually to the point. Being in a partnership with someone from Emilia Romagna the other side of the huge sliding doors, the Epicurean delights can continue through the evening, enjoyed of course for their own sake but also crucially keeping him healthy. In the food and wine new thoughts arise, new information is imparted, new friends and contacts may be made, to be of some help some time. If you can catch him at dinner you will see that he is always alert, if silent. The battle against compunction is never won, and is never lost either.

His life is a structure of anti-formalism built as a defence against the closing of the mind. He wears simple comfortable faded-cotton work clothes with no concessions to conventional formality - the opposite end of the scale to the sharp-suited and scented account executive, who has everything to hide. There was one suit, bought in the 1960s and re-tailored umpteen times as demanded by the changes inside it and outside it. Not many have seen it; it has gained mythical status. Not many saw what the old guard changed into when he went to Buckingham Palace to meet the Duke and receive an institutional pat on the back. He is distrusting, if not fearful, of pomp. But he has his own pride. He knows how far he has come. And sometimes he expects others to know it. This is the pride, which is part of, and defines, the humility. It will sometimes, very rarely, poke through the self effacement. A young man once asked him 'Who the hell do you think you are?' and he said 'I am the man at the top of the tree.' But the young man said 'Which tree? There are so many in the wood.' But he will not get into an argument on such terms. If he thinks you are wrong, he says 'It's up to you.' If he thinks you are right, he says 'Let me think about it.'

Explaining himself is not something he has ever regarded as important. Earlier in his life he made his choices about directions and attitudes. Looking for lost 'innocence' and the 'essence of being' is not too bad an excuse for a life. In Spain, in America, in Venezuela, in Italy he fuelled his beliefs. In England he let himself run, always on the look-out. To keep the search going requires some obstinacy, habituation and tenacity. His temperament would have made him a good playwright or even a clever young mathematician. Graphic design happened to suit his talents.

Regretting little, perhaps only letting slip a few opportunities through what he regards as his laziness - and some of these are still secret and will always remain so - he now feels confident enough to tell you what he likes, not dwelling on what he doesn't like. He likes what he sees. If you were to ask him to contemplate anathema it would be to ask him simply to stop looking. Because without light he would lose the means to keep himself away from everything that could corrupt his idea of life. With nothing to see there would be little scope for him to remain free, free of definition, free of category, and even free of obligation. By looking around, even when he is asleep, he has become a master of the art of living, at least of his own life, and has also become a mark of history. There is a piece of his work whose form, style, irony and pleasure signify much of his particular art and distinction, and thus his achievement. It was not done for a commission. It was done recently for himself, and for this book. It simply designs the word 'Daydreams'.

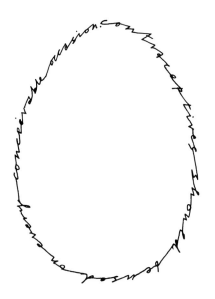

Wroughting and wrighting

According to designer Bruce Archer's great aunt the catchy phrase **the three Rs** – reading, writing and 'rithmetic – was

coined in the early nineteenth century by an illiterate member of Parliament speaking on an issue of education. This

phrase, the great aunt maintained, was a misquotation of an earlier aphorism: **reading and writing, reckoning and**

figuring, wroughting and wrighting. From **reading and writing** we get **literacy**, and from **reckoning and figuring**

comes **numeracy**, but there is no equivalent word for the result of **wroughting and wrighting** – the creation and making

of things. At one time back in the 1950s there was an effort to introduce the term **technics** but the only word in current

use which gets anywhere near is **Design**. Spelt with a capital **D**. The word is often used incorrectly and the habit of

labelling a finished product as a **Design**, rather than a thinking **process**, is quite wrong:

Design is intelligence made visible.

(Acknowledgement to Bruce Archer, AF)

'You can't actually draw sunshine – you can only imply it.' This section attempts to register the sensations of weather, humidity and temperature, using just pen and pencil, ink and paper.

With these basic implements, Fletcher manages to make us feel a breeze, warmth, piercing cold, or pervading damp. So abstract are some of the visualizations, taken from a calendar of 'Unreliable seasonal predictions', that they remind us that all visual art requires the active participation of the viewer, and a willingness to engage with the proposition being communicated.

Not an unreasonable expectation, as he points out, since 'in conversation you have to listen as well as talk'.

For March, Fletcher scratched down sleet as sharp aggressive lines. Then he threw water over the artwork so that it looked as though it had rained on the page. To express the lush green promise of May, he took a house painter's brush to make a wide expanse of verdant optimism and convey the sense of something beginning. The bright glow of the July sun is achieved by dropping a blob of orange ink onto dampened paper so that it diffused with a fuzzy halo. The heat of an August holiday is expressed by a tear providing the froth as the blue waves hit the blinding yellow sand. The colder, clearer days of September are represented by birds migrating across the blue sky. Fletcher found this month the hardest to resolve, yet in many ways, this is the most successful evocation in the calendar. October's autumnal leaves were made by tearing up brown envelopes containing bills, tax demands and other unfriendly notifications suggesting the onset of winter. Foggy November days are expressed by pencil shading so impenetrable that it almost obscures the dates. The chilly snow of December is evoked by printing his thumbprints in clear transparent varnish.

May

M	T	W	T	F	S	S
6	7	1	2	3		
13	14	8	9	10	4	5
20	21	15	16	17	11	12
27	28	22	23	24	18	19
		29	30	31	25	26

A blazing July

A hot day on the beach... and a fresh September morning

August
M T W T F S S
       1 2 3 4
5 6 7 8 9 10 11
12 13 14 15 16 17 18
19 20 21 22 23 24 25
26 27 28 29 30 31

Autumn leaves

November fog

November
M T W T F S S
            1 2 3
4 5 6 7 8 9 10
11 12 13 14 15 16 17
18 19 20 21 22 23 24
25 26 27 28 29 30 -

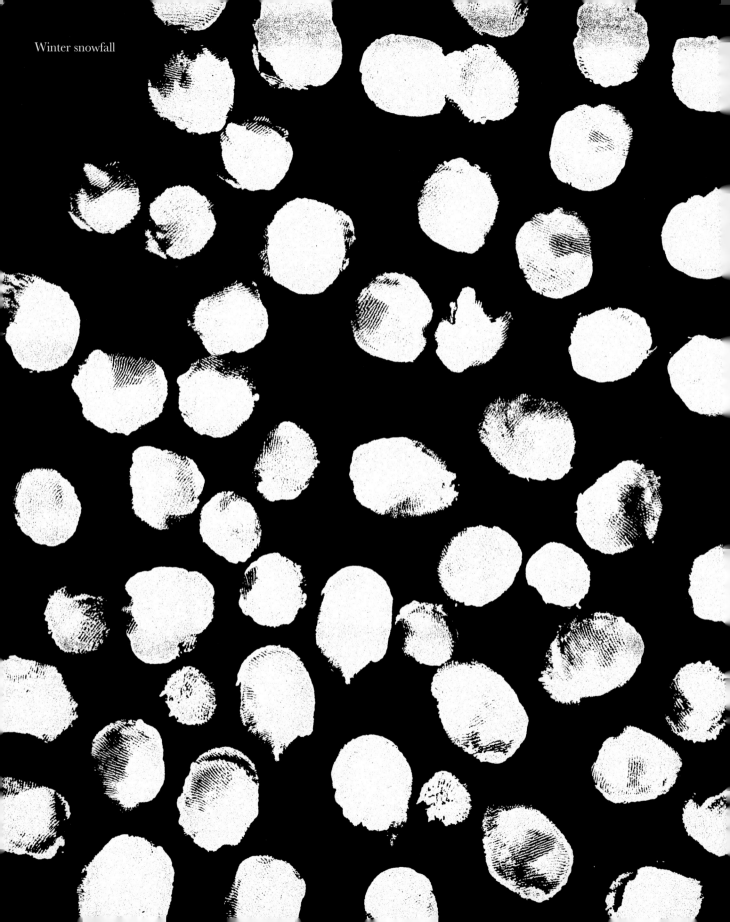

Winter snowfall

Apollinaire said that one can paint with pipes, stamps, postcards or playing cards, candlesticks, waxed cloth, collars, painted paper and newspapers. The same principle applies to making graphic messages.

. Purloining

Alan Fletcher is not averse to pilfering – even from within his own portfolio. He may refurbish an old idea or improve on it, or treat it in a new way. Whatever the case and whether copying or borrowing or stealing, it's always done for a purpose.

The poster (below) reproduces a facsimile international street sign, providing a perfect acquisition (or flagrant act) to make a counterpoint to Jerome K Jerome's comment and establish the contradiction between the visual warning and the verbal declaration – two stolen items combining to sharpen the sentiment that they each express.

" I like work–it fascinates me– I can sit and look at it for hours"

Copying can be taken to extremes. Here are two.

The cover of a paperback book which is intended to
simulate the bold appearance of an early nineteenth-
century placard. A pastiche of xerox-copied letters
of the era pasted-up into a typical layout of the period.
The poor quality of the artwork contributes to the
desired effect.

A less obvious approach was used on this poster for
the architect Emilio Ambasz. According to Fletcher,
the thought for this design occurred to him after reading
that for the traditional Japanese master wood engraver,
the ultimate skill lay in rendering the face of a Geisha
girl as seen through a mosquito net – a skill he evidently
appreciates, but can only try and emulate. Anyway
the skill in this poster lies in making the picture the
information, with Ambasz peering adroitly through
a screen of the information and his own *curriculum vitae*.

EMILIO AMBASZ • ARCHITECT/DESIGNER • THE ANNUAL PENTAGRAM LECTURE
TO BE HELD BY THE DESIGN MUSEUM AT THE ROYAL GEOGRAPHICAL SOCIETY
• 1 KENSINGTON GORE, LONDON SW7 • WEDNESDAY 20 MAY 1992 • LECTURE
7.00 TO 8.15 • RECEPTION 8.15 TO 9.15 • TICKETS £15 • CONCESSIONS £10
FROM THE DESIGN MUSEUM, BUTLERS WHARF, SHAD THAMES, LONDON SE1 2YD,
TELEPHONE (071) 403 6933 FROM 9.30AM TO 5.30 WEEKDAYS • FAX (071)
378 6540 WEEKENDS • EMILIO AMBASZ: WAS BORN IN ARGENTINA 1943 •
MASTER'S IN ARCHITECTURE AT PRINCETON   UNIVERSITY • TAUGHT AT
PRINCETON UNIVERSITY SCHOOL OF ARCHITECTURE • CURATOR OF DESIGN,
THE MUSEUM OF MODERN ART, NEW YORK (1970/76) • DIRECTED NUMEROUS
INFLUENTIAL EXHIBITS ON ARCHITECTURE AND INDUSTRIAL DESIGN, AMONG
THEM "ITALY, THE NEW DOMESTIC LANDSCAPE" (1972) • "THE ARCHITECTURE
OF LUIS BARRAGAN" (1974) • THE TAXI PROJECT (1976) • PRESIDENT OF THE
ARCHITECTURAL LEAGUE (1981/85) • VISITING PROFESSOR AT HOCHSCHULE
FUR GESTALTUNG, ULM • CHIEF DESIGN CONSULTANT, CUMMINS ENGINE CO.
• ARCHITECTURE: MUSEUM OF AMERICAN FOLK ART, NEW YORK CITY • GRAND
RAPIDS ART MUSEUM • CONSERVATORY, SAN ANTONIO BOTANICAL CENTRE •
INTERIORS: BANQUE BRUXELLES LAMBERT IN LAUSANNE, MILAN, NEW YORK
• HEADQUARTERS FOR THE FINANCIAL GUARANTY INSURANCE COMPANY, NEW YORK •
MERCEDES-BENZ SHOWROOM • PLANNING: SCHLUMBERGER TOWER,
FRANKFURT • OTHER PROJECTS • EXPO '92, SEVILLE, REPRESENTED
USA. VENICE BIENNALE • INDUSTRIAL DESIGN • DESIGN OF VERTEBRA
SEATING SYSTEM • ARPE DESK LUMINAIRE SPOTLIGHT • LOGOTEC
SPOTIGHT • OSERIS SPOTLIGHT • GISEULA LINEAR LIGHTING
SYSTEM • VITERBE SANITARY FITTINGS • DIESEL ENGINE •
AQUACOLOR WATERCOLOUR SET • SELECTED EXHIBITIONS:
AXIS GALLERY, TOKYO • LEO CASTELLI GALLERY,
NEW YORK • THE MUSEUM OF MODERN ART,
NEW YORK • THE PHILADELPHIA
• LA JOLLA MUSEUM OF CONTEMPORARY
ART, CALIFORNIA • THE AKRON ART
MUSEUM • DESIGN OF THE CENTRE OF CONTEMPORARY ART
IN BORDEAUX • SCULPTURE PARK, ST LOUIS • TRAVELLING EXHIBIT
MILAN, MADRID, TOKYO • AWARDS: THE IBD GOLD MEDAL, USA (1977)
• SMAU PRIZE, MILAN • PROGRESSIVE ARCHITECTURE AWARDS (1976,
1980, 1985) • ANNUAL AWARDS (1983) • AMERICAN INSTITUTE OF
ARCHITECTS (1976) • GRAND
PRIZE, INTERNATIONAL • COMPASSO D'ORO,
ITALY (1987) • ID AWARDS
(1980, 1987, 1989) • MAGAZINES WITH
SPECIAL ISSUES • ARCHITECTURISM • DOMUS •
SPACE AND DESIGN • MONOGRAPH •
MANY OF HIS DESIGNS IN COLLECTIONS OF THE
MUSEUM OF MODERN ART, NEW YORK •

How to play **the environment game**
An Arts Council exhibition which explains the theory, stakes, ploys and gambits which are manipulating and corroding our environment.
12 April to 24 June 1973. Monday to Friday 10.00 to 20.00. Saturday 10.00 to 18.00. Sunday 12.00 to 18.00.
Admission 30p (Mondays 10p). Hayward Gallery, South Bank.

It is acceptable to steal, providing you don't pass the idea off as your own – that's plagiarism. At least that's Alan Fletcher's opinion. The design of this object (left) was adapted from a Victorian device for holding envelopes. The base was a similar shape but the original had two wooden cylinders to grip the envelopes. These were substituted with two stainless steel ball bearings, which could revolve in all directions and were heavier, and introduced a lateral groove into the curved wooden base to keep them on track. 'I felt it was a substantial improvement,' he says, 'but they cost a fortune to make, so weren't a great commercial success.' The value of ideas is obviously relative to their cost.

The book jacket steals Monopoly houses to build a skyscraper. A neat conversion of the suburban into the urban, a visual synopsis of the debate contained in the publication.

This man celebrated the 21st anniversary dinner of
D&AD, the Design and Art Directors' Association.
In fact he was borrowed from a Cassandre drawing
of a man in a bathing suit which featured in a famous
series of advertisements for Dubonnet in the 1930s.
Fletcher called Dubonnet in Paris to ask permission
to reproduce the famous character. But, they said they
had never heard of the designer nor did they recollect
the character. Nevertheless, they said reproducing the
design would infringe copyright and withheld their
permission. Undeterred, Fletcher went ahead and
redressed him in a blue suit and bowler hat, so that
he was appropriately turned out for the occasion, and
inserted the line 'Homage to Cassandre' running down
his trouser leg.

Overleaf

But if borrowing from others is one thing, borrowing
from yourself is another. Asked to contribute a poster
design for the Mexican Biennale, to commemorate the
500th anniversary of the discovery of the New World
by Columbus, Fletcher decided to recycle (or borrow)
a design he'd done for an earlier (unpaid) project.
'I felt that it was even more suitable,' he says. Which
only goes to show that sometimes a solution for one
problem can be a better one for another. Or that some
ideas are solutions in search of a problem.

The intention was that the undulating lines, to give
an impression of the swell of the sea, should not touch.
He started drawing them on a quiet Sunday afternoon
but by the time he was three-quarters of the way
through, he usually had to stop for a rest and a drink.
When he resumed, he inevitably made a mistake, and
had to start all over again – and again. It took several
Sunday afternoons to get it right, but by then he'd
decided that the odd mistake emphasized his original
intention. An overwhelming compulsion to achieve
perfection can preclude creativity.

D&AD
21ST

DESIGN & ART DIRECTORS ASSOCIATION · 21ST ANNIVERSARY · AWARDS DINNER · 8 JUNE '83 · ROYAL ALBERT HALL · LONDON ·

A view of the New World as seen by Columbus at 2 am on the 12th October 1492

Style is the particular in spite of the general - the difference between Howard Keel and Ray Charles singing *Some Enchanted Evening*. Style amplifies content with personality. At its best it has panache and a confidence in expression: Greta Garbo or the Bugatti Roadster. At its worst it is merely mannerism. A confection, a snail in puff pastry.

I had an acquaintance who held me personally responsible (as a designer) for the inadequacies of his smart Italian lamp. His frustration centred on changing the light bulb which required several screwdrivers, electrical pliers, an extra pair of hands and probably several hours of frustration. By directing his irritation towards me he was expressing the deeply rooted belief that design is synonymous with style. Actually the reverse is true because the stylist only disguises the degree to which a problem was not solved, rather than the degree to which it was.

The original mind aims for the centre but the stylist can only rework the circumference. Locked into a repetitive mode they usually end up a victim of their trademark. Do you know about the sea squirt? This roams the sea seeking a rock to cling to for the rest of its life; when it finds one, it no longer needs its brain, so eats it.

AF

Most corporate identity programmes make a virtue of uniform application. However, that often leads to dull, monotonous work rigidly policed by rulebooks and manuals, which remain unloved, unread and on the shelf. But, as this section demonstrates, it is possible to treat uniformity in a way which leads to more lively solutions. Experience, however, has taught Fletcher that this approach rarely works. 'Most clients can't be bothered to drive an identity,' he regretfully concludes, 'they just want to rubber-stamp everything.'

Nevertheless, he prefers to express an organization's personality, rather than simply record it through a static trademark. Whether by inventing an articulated macquette, or by exploiting the potential of modular units, or by extending the influence of an identity through a souvenir. These are just a few of the ways he goes about it.

Sometimes it's not a choice, it's a legal requirement. An identity for the international accountants and management consultants, Arthur Andersen & Co., had to conform to differing national legislations by including different suffixes. The solution lay in giving an ampersand an elongated sweep to encompass these variations.

Renowned for its vast beer consumption, the Munich *Oktoberfest* is in fact the largest folk festival in the world with its origins in the wedding ceremony held in 1810 of Prince Ludwig of Bavaria and Princess Therese von Sachsen-Hildburghansen. With three and a half million annual visitors, the Munich breweries erect vast tents (the largest holds well over 10,000 people) and some 10 million litres of beer are consumed over the two weeks of festivities.

The commission for this symbol arrived in the best possible way. A local entrepreneur had designed and registered an unofficial symbol, and no doubt was anticipating a handsome financial reward. However, the Tourist Office, suddenly aware of what would be a lost opportunity, immediately decided they had to have an official symbol designed and quickly.

The visual associations connected with the festival range from pretzels to sausages, gingerbread hearts to folk costumes, but the most common have to be the steins of beer. The solution speaks for itself. However, the extension of symbol to product introduces a new notion into the vocabulary of corporate identity. The sketch schematic models combining different expressions (opposite) were those used to present the scheme.

Compare the thinking with the faces used on other jobs shown on pages 80, 81, 166 and 167.

OKTOBERFEST

Articulated emblems

Black Sun are corporate publishers. They conceive, write, illustrate, design and produce annual reports, facility brochures and technical literature. Their emblem has five separate elements, all of which can contribute to changes of expression. They can register smiles or frowns, be quizzical or questioning, look happy or miserable, all according to the context in which they appear – a character intended to look as if it was doodled directly onto the paper.

As a tyre company, Pirelli envied Bibendum, the Michelin Man, an advertising personality known around the world. Pirelli wanted a similar figure to promote their products and asked Fletcher to come up with someone. He invented the Pirelliman, an articulated macquette which could twist and turn, adopt different poses and travel in all directions. The macquette was sent out to Pirelli's worldwide network of advertising agents in a box. The symbol worked for a while but then the agencies complained he always looked as if he was going to fall over. He was made redundant.

   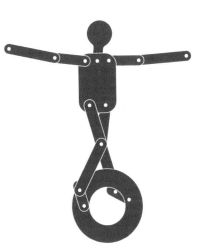

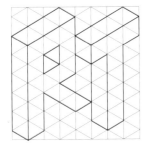

The potential of existing modular systems can be seen in the two examples shown. The emblem for a firm of architects, Rock Townsend, was based on a standard graph paper in the same way as mediaeval stonemasons based their marks on the geometric matrix of their guild. The linear grid was used to outline the initials of the firm as well as those of the individual partners.

The discovery of a modular typeface in an Italian type specimen book led to this style of logotype (opposite) for Design Systems, a company which manufactures queuing and routing systems. Working with the set of twenty units, the company initials could appear fat or thin, tall or short, condensed or expanded. This design reflected the flexible attributes of the products and the engineering precision the company was seeking to promote. The typeface is called *Fregio Mecano*. It can also be found, paradoxically, in an unflexible version, in computer software. Under another name, of course.

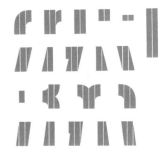

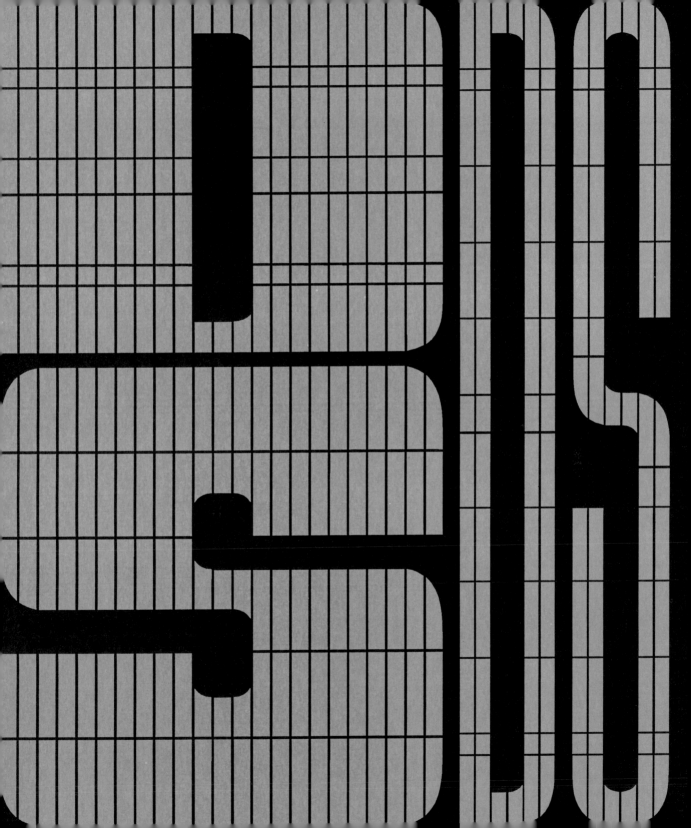

The Santa Barbara Museum of Art in California, on their 50th anniversary, decided to update their identity and house style. Fletcher proposed that they should audaciously hijack the word 'Art' and created fifteen different emblems, some of which are shown here. To extend the range he proposed that each successive year they should ask other designers to contribute to the 'Art' collection. The emblems represent the range of artefacts and collections housed in the Museum. Different designs were intended to stand for different departments, different collections and different events.

The objective was to project the museum as an active rather than a passive institution. However, art doesn't always conquer all. The arrival of a new director with other opinions during the implementation of the scheme resulted in emasculation. One design (opposite) was adopted and the rest binned. At least, that was the last Fletcher heard.

Overleaf

Dozens of early sketches were generated in the search for an uninhibited and painterly rendition of the word. Here are a few.

SANTA BARBARA MUSEUM OF ART

try.
otive soc
ot exempt
Or Hahn believe
scious of its res-
society and the

ribution is Fu-
hicle which
echnology.
ulating glass
cent of the
divided into
lower sec-
to the sills.
ystem is
nsors
o park
avail-
ation
splays
ra's
h
hani-
as
ar.

nes
to comp
although th
sion on the stock

When Discovery g
here in mid-November,
priced at around £16,000, whi
may tempt some would-be Ra
Rover buyers. They may also
tempted by the new 2.5 litre d
engine which Land Rover has
veloped to power Discovery in
dition to the 3.5 litre V8 petrol
engine. With the optional in
facing rear seats, Discove
provide seven seats wit
which will appeal to
school run. Initial
will build 200 ve
rising to 300
which mus
even at t

There is a sequence of stages between facing out a problem and arriving at an acceptable solution. The initial step is getting the bits and pieces into some order to point up the kernel of the issue. The next move is to head off along the most likely route. The outcome of this excursion may be instantly evident, or more likely lead to an exasperating period of hiatus when, despite trying this and that, the answer remains elusive. Hopefully, after a while, the germ of an idea eventually peeps through. However, before leaping on it with relief my inclination is to let it incubate for a while. Here the mind works on it in some mysterious way. Either its potential evaporates, in which case one has to start all over again, or it emerges with a 'firm iridescent surface, and a notable increase in weight'.

AF

Negative is positive

To Alan Fletcher's mind, the hole is as important as the doughnut. This section shows how negative shapes can be of as much use as the positive forms, or how positive statements can be negative, and vice versa. This may be applied to the figurative or abstract, or through light and shade, or by shadow and substance.

Take the logotype for a private informal supper club for architects and critics. They call themselves the 'Philistines' – as that's how they feel they would be regarded by traditionalists. The solution plays with a double negative – the Roman letters representing classical precepts defaced by a graffiti hooligan.

These designs play with implied form. The image of a shaving mirror was contrived for a manufacturer of metal foil. The mirror was reproduced stamped in silver and the profile of the man shaving belongs to the technician who did the mechanical.

The *Domus* cover (opposite) plays on a double meaning in that articles profiling architects are frequently run as editorial features. The illustration revisits the famous Marcel Duchamp self-portrait. Many other designers have performed the same act of homage (or theft) in their various diverse ways, but Fletcher's contribution is to suggest a colourful and vibrant personality.

The profile of a lady (below), cut out of each item in a range of stationery, was the physical identity of a photographer's representative.

Min Hogg represents
Brian Morris, Ray Rathborne,
and Richard Yeend from
24 Rupert Street, London W1V 7FN
Telephone 01 437 5062

The announcement of a two-day public viewing of
private grand palazzi and art collections in Naples uses
the idea of peeping through a keyhole. The solution was
partly arrived at through word association (door, closed,
locked, keyhole) and partly through visual association
(keyhole, chess pawn and – enlarged – a monument).
The negative shape of the keyhole is mirrored by the
positive shape of the monument. One piece of artwork
also served for each half – a positive aspect of both
visual and printing economy.

A poster is, however, only as effective as its application
and the environment in which it is posted. As you can
see from the photograph, this is an example of how
positive can easily become negative. By the way the
adjacent notice states that the building is a school,
and the porter will immediately call the police if there
is any sign of drug activity.

Monumenti Porte Aperte

Napoli 9/10 Maggio 1992

An Easter card for an Italian company utilizes a tonal relationship between light to dark to produce an egg. A powerful poster for IBM makes a rhetorical bridge between darkness and light, despair and hope.

light
a candle

'Art does not

reproduce the visible

rather it makes visible'.

Paul Klee

In the poster shown opposite, the shadows echo the sentiment of the saying and were scribbled to reflect its reference to art.

The vignette (below) illustrated a magazine article on the need for a move away from transience towards more durability in architecture. This current debate is graphically highlighted by implying that a thin panel has the potential to be a substantial cube. Implication can often communicate more than description.

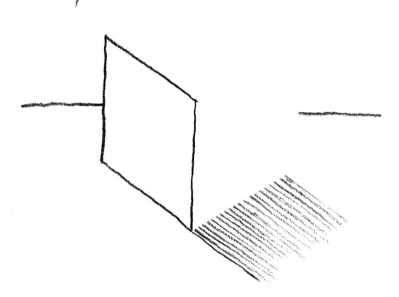

Overleaf

How to show the white cliffs of Dover without actually drawing them. The green clifftop was a dribble of ink. The turbulent sea was created by rough strokes of the front and back of a pen.

The white cliffs of Dover

Blue skies & GREY BOXES

Basically there are two kinds of designer:

Helicopters and VENDING MACHINES.

The helicopters fly around the l a n d s c a p e

zooming in to investigate, backing off to get a better panoramic view.

On the other hand VENDING MACHINES tend to be INERT

until someone shoves money in the slot.

They then produce a lot of buzzing, WHIRRING and clanking,

until out pops a PRODUCT.

It is invariably the same as the previous one, and will be the same as the next.

The only difference is the next is usually staler.

Traditional illustrations of the signs of the Zodiac are often overworked and sentimental. Alan Fletcher gave himself the challenge of addressing these symbols more vigorously by emphasizing the essence of what they are intended to represent. Virgo, for instance, was rendered as a nun. Fletcher used only scissors, coloured papers, and pen – and, of course, no little imagination. These designs populated a calendar on the Zodiac.

It was a matter of trial and error as he improvised his way towards each characterization. Thus the use of legal seals to give the scuttling crab (Cancer) serrated pincers and claws.

Some of the other signs shown are accompanied by the sketches which informed their development, or, in the case of Taurus (the Bull), accompanied by a collage elaborated at a later date from the image produced for the calendar. Again the formalizations demonstrate his ability to characterize by implication rather than by representation.

Taurus the bull

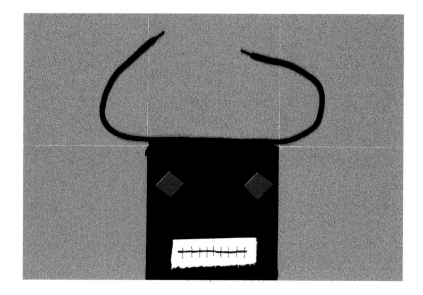

This one-off design was developed from the calendar
image of Taurus (opposite) for a friend's 50th birthday.
It was compiled from sandpaper, shoelaces, hide, tape,
paper and staples. Another example of how one thing
can sometimes lead to another.

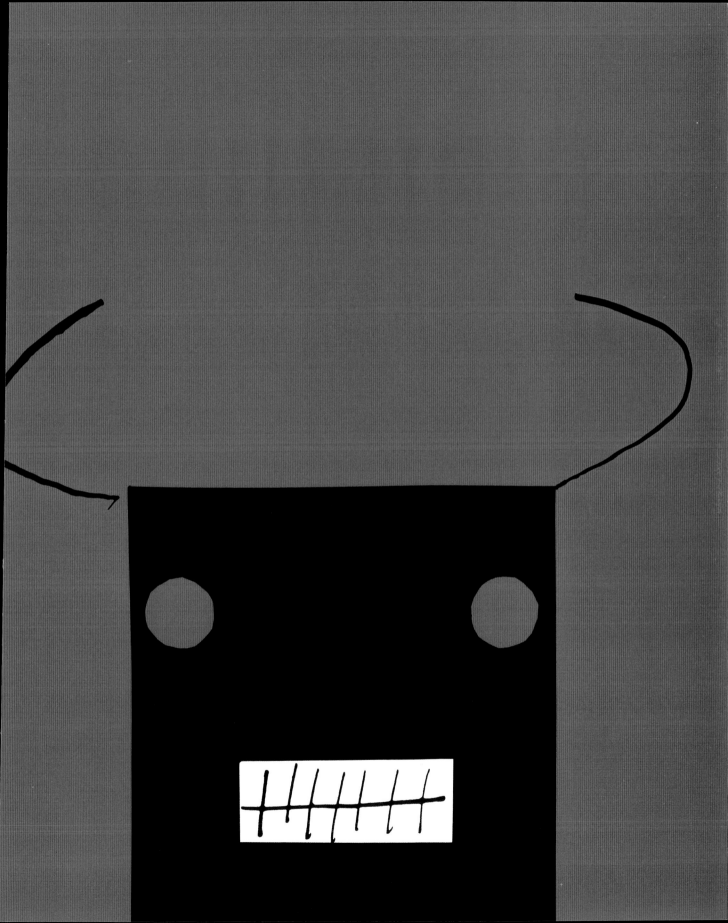

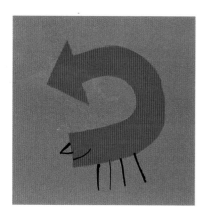

Scorpio the scorpion

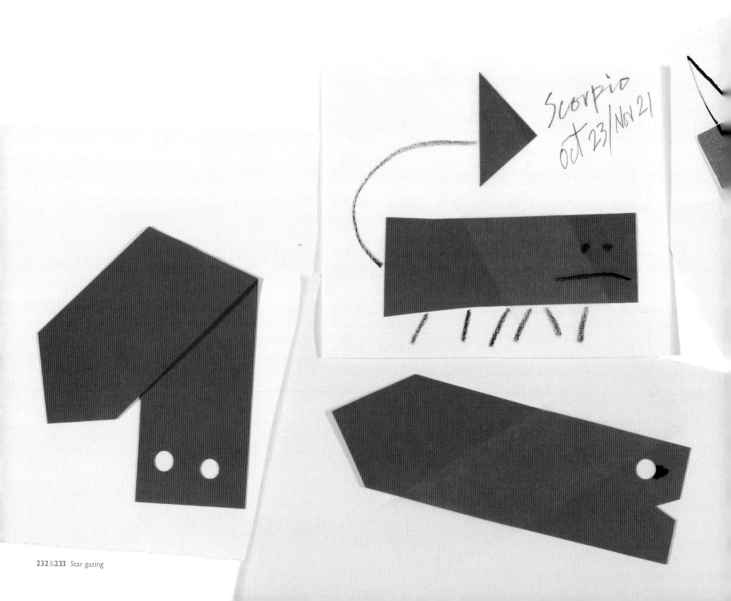

Scorpio
Oct 23/Nov 21

Capricorn the goat

Aquarius the water carrier

Aquarius the water carrier

PANTONE® 313 U

320 U

Virgo the virgin

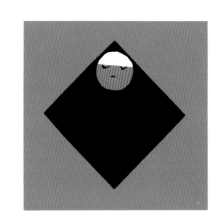

Virgo the Virgin

Aries the ram

A typeface is an alphabet in a straitjacket

For Alan Fletcher typefaces are raw material. They are malleable forms which can be made into anything, from yachts to portraits, or manipulated to express a sentiment, or even to have a party. This section looks at how he juggles with type to shape some unusually appropriate solutions.

The visual device below was a project for a section heading for a gossip column (*Über Leute* – about people) in *Frankfurter Allgemeine* magazine. Here the U represents the face, the L the nose and the exclamation mark both mouth and speech balloon. A combination that also captures the personality of the gossip-monger.

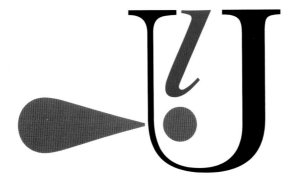

A pair of gates

Fletcher had a pair of large ordinary wrought iron gates at the entrance to his house. For years he'd toyed with the idea of replacing them with the alphabet translated into elongated metal letters to form the bars and rails. Eventually he got round to doing the design, made a sketch, and sent it off to a craftsman for an estimate.

At about the same time, the two brick pillars which supported the gates collapsed, and the gates were lifted off their hinges so that the pillars could be rebuilt. No sooner were they set on the ground than they were stolen. They were so heavy that there must have been at least three men to lift them and a flatbed truck to take them away. The insurance claim was submitted with an estimate (from the same craftsman) for making a pair of gates identical to the ones which had been stolen. The insurance company accepted the cost and paid up. He then had his own version made, which coincidentally cost exactly the same as the pair of original gates.

The alphabet was derived from a Victorian condensed wood typeface and amended to accommodate the requirements of metal and to achieve the density of bar and rail. The pair of gates is split between the M and the N; the tail of the Q functions as the gate stop. They are seven feet high and are mounted on large hinges to swing like barn doors – they can't be unhinged.

When Daimler Benz held a competition to celebrate
the 100th anniversary of the automobile, Fletcher's
deceptively simple idea – to create an automobile from
100 by tilting the 1 and using the zeros as wheels – won
joint first prize. He had the copyline printed in yellow
– to reflect London's 'no parking' lines – a decidedly
British private joke.

The seeming effortlessness of the solution, though, masks
the geometric construction that post-rationalized the
design. The calculations exactly match the design,
a fact which he found both pleasing and surprising.

Incidentally this was one project which really paid –
and paid – and paid. As Fletcher recalls: 'I was one
of six paid to enter the competition. Then I won half
the prize money. Then they wanted to use the design
as a promotional emblem worldwide – so I got paid
again. Then they wanted the copyright – so I was paid
for a fourth time.' Not bad for someone who is not
even interested in cars. (He has a Mini Moke, but
prefers to take a cab.)

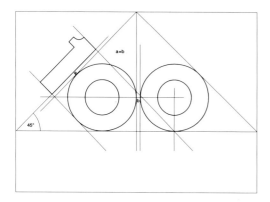

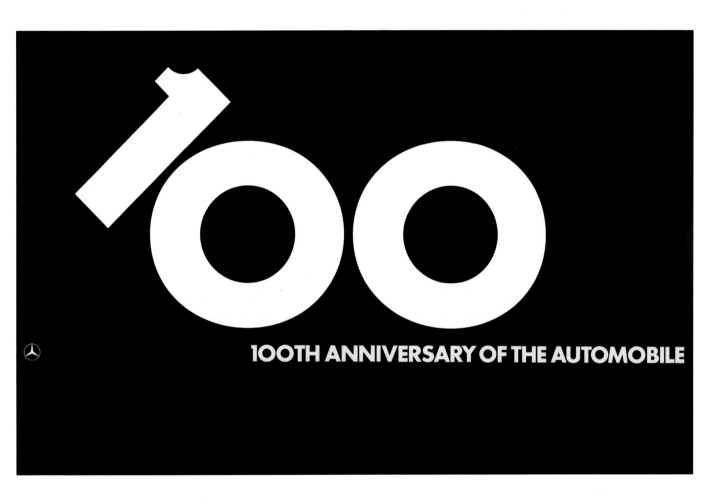

100TH ANNIVERSARY OF THE AUTOMOBILE

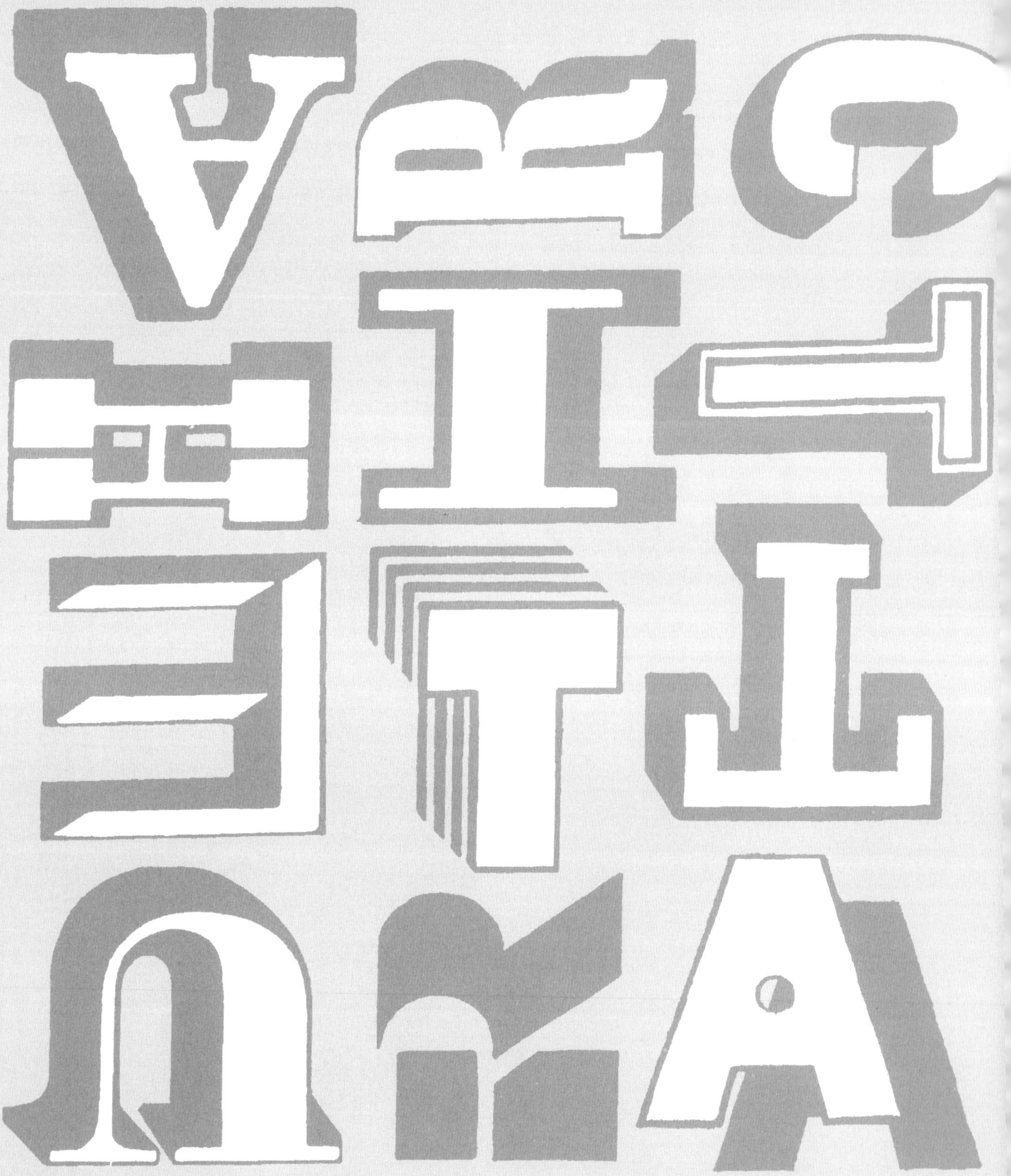

Type as a metaphor

Inventive interrelationships can create visual effects which resonate far beyond the literal meaning. The letter composition of a logo for Fire and Iron, a crafts gallery of metalwork, not only spells the name but also evokes the glowing coals and heat of the blacksmith's furnace. The craftsman is the very same one who made the pair of gates (see page 240).

Richard Rogers Partnership

Richard Rogers
John Young
Marco Goldschmied
Michael Davies

Lawrence Abbott
Pierre Botschi
Lennart Grut
Amarjit Kalsi
Graham Stirk

Thames Wharf, Rainville Road
London W6 9HA
Telephone 071 385 1235
Fascimile 071 385 8409
Telex 887126

Simply standing type on its end can hint at a skyline, as in this image used on a stationery range for an architect. But type can go even further and produce an entire alphabetical city, as portrayed by the aerial view of a downtown district shown opposite. An invitation for a friend's 21st birthday party captures the informality of the occasion by the intimate intertwining and vibrant deconstruction of the word.

"Every work of art
is a child of its time."
—Wassily Kandinsky

The poster design on the left interprets the spirit of the words supplied by Kandinsky. The T evokes a column, whereas the traditional German letter style of the R, by being tipped forward to stand on one leg, suggests a posturing sculpture. The inverted A might be a bird, or helmet, or no more than a whimsical notion.

The K for the annual regatta held in Kiel, Germany, becomes a white yacht sailing across a rich dark blue sea. Note the simple tear to indicate the froth of the wake. Commissioned to submit a design by the city as one of four designers in a limited competition, the jurors either considered his design inappropriate, or thought that it wouldn't be readily understood, or preferred one of the other submissions, or perhaps they just didn't like it. Anyway the poster was rejected.

MARIO BELLINI,
ARCHITECT/DESIGNER
GIVES THE FIRST ANNUAL
PENTAGRAM LECTURE. THE
DESIGN MUSEUM 22 MAY 1991.
WEDNESDAY FROM 7.30 TO 9PM.
TICKETS £10, CONCESSIONS £7.50,
FROM THE DESIGN MUSEUM
BUTLERS WHARF, LONDON
SE1 2YD. TELEPHONE:
071 403 6933 BETWEEN
9.30/5.30 WEEKDAYS,
OR FAX 071 378 6540.
MARIO BELLINI IS
AN ARCHITECT AND
PRODUCT DESIGNER OF
ENORMOUS RANGE AND VARIETY:
THE TOKYO DESIGN CENTRE, A MAJOR
EXPANSION OF THE SITE OF THE MILAN FAIR.
THE CAB CHAIR FOR CASSINA. THE PERSONA AND
FIGURA OFFICE CHAIRS FOR VITRA. THE DIVISUMMA
LOGOS CALCULATORS AND THE ETP 55 TYPEWRITER
FOR OLIVETTI, FOR WHOM HE HAS BEEN CONSULTANT
SINCE 1962. MEMBER OF THE EXECUTIVE COMMITTEE
OF THE MILAN TRIENNALE IN 1986. PLANNED THE HUGE
PROGETTO DOMESTICO EXHIBITION. EDITOR OF DOMUS.
HE HAS WON NUMEROUS AWARDS: THE COMPASSO D'ORO
IN ITALY, THE ANNUAL AWARD IN THE USA, THE MADE IN
GERMANY AWARD, THE GOLD MEDAL IN SPAIN. TWENTY
OF HIS DESIGNS ARE IN THE PERMANENT COLLECTION OF
THE MUSEUM OF MODERN ART IN NEW YORK, WHERE AN
EXHIBITION DEVOTED TO HIS WORK WAS HELD IN 1987.

Fletcher's interest in ideograms, in which words form pictures, is evident in these examples. The calligraphic emblem for Pavitts Products, purveyors of fruit and vegetables, becomes an apple. In the ideogram to promote a lecture by architect Mario Bellini, all the information composes his portrait. A practical consideration here was that the same piece of artwork could be used to reproduce a poster, leaflet and ticket. The glass, which was for an importer of wine and champagne, was borrowed from an eighteenth-century ideogram of a French drinking song. By simply adding three lines of type he tops up the glass to include the client.

John Elliott Cellars Ltd, 11 Dover Street,
Mayfair, London. Telephone: 01 493 5135
Wholesalers of Fine Wines & Champagne
Buvons, amis, et buvons à plein verre.
Enivrons-nous de ce nectar divin!
Après les Belles, sur la terre,
Rien n'est aimable que le vin;
Cette liqueur est de tout âge:
Buvons-en! Nargue du sage
Qui, le verre en main,
Le haussant soudain,
Craint, se ménage,
Et dit : holà!
Trop cela!
Holà!
La!
La!
La!
Car
Panard
A pour refrain:
Tout plein!
Plein!
Plein!
Plein!
Fêtons,
Célébrons
Sa mémoire;
Et, pour sa gloire,
Rions, chantons, aimons, buvons.

Letterboxes

Alan Fletcher the graphic designer turns his skill to working in three dimensions with a series of three desktop boxes, each about 12 inches (30 cm) high. They were made for an exhibition of innovative products mounted by Zeev Aram, the pioneering designer and retailer. Once again we see an enjoyment of puns, letters, numbers and objects, things which live in their own right. The letterboxes, comprising drawers, slides, lids and containers, proved diabolically expensive to make. 'Most of my work is either ridiculously cheap or outrageously expensive,' comments Fletcher. So what's new?

Alan Fletcher belongs to that élite international group of designers who have transcended the conventional boundaries of their craft. In a long and distinguished career, he has been associated with some of the most progressive patrons of modern design, including Reuters, Lloyd's of London, IBM, Herman Miller, Olivetti, Pirelli, *Fortune* and *Domus* magazines. He has tackled every facet of design – from corporate identities, sign programmes, calendars, books, newspapers, technical literature, to toys, desktop products and posters – with a style and a purpose that has marked him out as one of the most admired designers of his generation. There is perhaps nobody else who inhabits the world of ideas and ironies, of wit and ambiguity in graphic design in quite the way he does.

The manner in which he has been described by his peers provides an insight into the special nature of his skill. Rick Poynor, editor of *Eye* magazine, once described him as 'a ringmaster of paradox'; and FHK Henrion, writing in *Top Graphic Design*, referred to the way that he is 'intrigued by visual ambiguities and paradoxes for their own sake, as well as in the practical design problems posed by clients.' Martin Pedersen, publisher of *Graphis* magazine, has said that 'Alan's work, like himself, is honest, fresh, tasteful, frank and imaginative'. When he received an honorary degree from the Royal College of Art, he was hailed by Professor Christopher Frayling as a 'magician' of graphic design – a reference to the Pentagram, a magical five-pointed star, which he and the four other founding partners of the famous design firm chose as a name in 1972, and also to the elusive qualities of the alchemist in his own designs.

Such accolades tend to make him uneasy, as do the honours and awards he has accumulated in recent years. He seems uncomfortable with his elevation to the role of doyen or design statesman, which is not surprising considering that his newest work is as fresh and as relevant as anything he has ever done. One also senses that he finds acid criticism easier to handle than the syrup of praise. He can be tolerant of others, but is always demanding of himself. Rarely satisfied with expedient solutions he is always willing (and able) to push himself that extra mile to make the designs work for him as well as the client. Fletcher's world is one of self-discipline and self-absorption. Yet a reputation for sleight of hand and eye, for clever, humorous, off-the-cuff solutions, for effortless problem-solving has followed him around ever since he broke out of the mould of Swiss Style – a school of design in which he was rigorously tutored and still admires – to largely redefine the contemporary art of graphic communication.

He is a dedicated and sometimes obsessive man, yet the image of graphic design playboy has attached itself and it is an irony of the kind that he himself enjoys setting up and can perhaps appreciate, knowing the hard work involved in communicating a sense of wit. As James Thurber once remarked 'humour is a very serious business'. In particular one quotation has echoed through Fletcher's career. 'Function is fine,' he once wrote, 'but solving the problem is not the problem. The real problem is to invest solutions with visual surprise and above all with wit.' And then he went on to declare, 'A smile is worth a thousand pictures.' Thus he has been depicted as the man who took all that serious less-is-more, form-follows-function dogma and somehow found a way to, well, *relax*.

Alan Fletcher is reticent about ascribing aspects of his creative approach to his background and upbringing. But there is no doubt that his early life provided many unusual influences. He was born in Nairobi, Kenya, in 1931, the son of an English civil servant. One of his earliest memories is of wearing a hat with a red handkerchief, which his mother had pinned to the back to protect his neck from the fierce sun. 'Wherever I went I was pursued by a red flapping cloth', he recalls. Somewhat surprisingly, to this day his favourite colour is red. Africa at that time was known as the 'white man's grave'. So it proved. When he was just five his father became terminally ill and the family returned to England by ship. On the way home, one night he saw what he thought were fireworks in the sky above the Straits of Gibraltar. It was in fact Franco's army crossing over from Morocco and signalling the start of the Spanish Civil War.

Back in London, he and his mother shared a gloomy house in Shepherds Bush with his grandfather, grandmother, two uncles and an aunt, and also his great-grandfather who had been born in 1843 – the roots of his childhood environment stretched as far back as the early Victorians. On his eighth birthday he recalls being issued with a gas mask in a local church crypt and, along with all the other schoolchildren, delighted in making rude noises by blowing through the flaps. He passed through the early part of the war collecting warm shrapnel on the way to school and studying the skyline for planes and barrage balloons. After the Blitz, he was sent to an academic and tough public boarding school called Christ's Hospital at Horsham. The uniform had not changed for 400 years and, as Fletcher grew, he was given someone else's hand-me-down gown, knee breeches, yellow stockings and shoes – 'I spent years wearing nothing else but a secondhand medieval costume,' he recollects.

Drawing. Barcelona 1952

Poster. Royal College of Art 1955

Advertising image of New York. Balding & Mansell 1957

At school, Fletcher failed to keep pace in academic subjects such as Maths and Latin, and took refuge in drawing. He also remembers being intrigued by the Dennis Wheatley murder-mystery books, which were presented in the manner of typescripts with facsimiles of letters, documents and tiny envelopes containing clues. He enjoyed copying the cartoons in back issues of *Punch*. When he became only the second person the school had ever allowed to sit for a certificate in art, he scored 98 per cent. This was perhaps not surprising since he confesses he was the only candidate. 'When I was leaving school,' says Fletcher, 'they asked how about working for a bank? That's where they sent second-level dum-dums. I said no. How about the army or navy? None of that. So what do you want to do? I said I'd like to go to art school. I couldn't think of anything else to suggest. They thought it was a frivolous ambition as well as socially dangerous.'

In fact Fletcher went to four art schools – Hammersmith, the Central School, the Royal College of Art, and, finally, Yale in the USA. He explains away this 'eternal-student' phase of his life with a characteristic shrug: 'I couldn't find any work, either as designer or road-digger, so I just kept applying for student grants.' A grant provided a basic sum of money to live on while studying. From Hammersmith, Fletcher transferred to the more vibrant creative atmosphere of the Central School where his fellow students in the early 1950s included Colin Forbes and Theo Crosby, both of whom were destined to become partners in Pentagram, as well as such future design luminaries as Derek Birdsall, Ken Garland, Terence Conran and David Hicks.

After graduating he still couldn't get work and a chance encounter led him to Spain where he taught English in Barcelona for a year. Fletcher was then accepted at the Royal College of Art (1953-6) where fellow students again proved an influence – Peter Blake, Len Deighton, David Gentleman, Malcolm Morely, Dick Smith and Joe Tilson among them. By the time he gained a scholarship to study in America at Yale University's School of Architecture and Design, he had been tutored by four of Britain's leading designers, illustrators and typographers – FHK Henrion, Paul Hogarth, Anthony Froshaug, and Herbert Spencer. But Yale introduced him to yet another roster of famous and influential designers who also taught: Alvin Eisenman, Norman Ives, Herbert Matter, Paul Rand, Bradbury Thompson, as well as the Bauhaus master Josef Albers.

America had emerged from the traumas of war with a powerful economy while Britain still remained deeply in hock; and had also provided a refuge for many of Europe's finest talents, whose skills contributed to the vigour of

Cover. *Fortune* magazine 1958

Promotional image. *Fortune* magazine 1959

Pencil pot. *Time & Life* magazine 1960

American design. To someone who had learnt about design in the grey austerity of Britain where commercial television did not go on air until 1955 and newsprint was rationed until 1956, America was a revelation.

'There were two jobs every young designer wanted to do in America at that time,' he recalls. 'One was to design a front cover for *Fortune* magazine and the other was to design an institutional advertisement for the Container Corporation' who, incidentally, had just started the annual Aspen Design Conference. He never managed to persuade the Container Corporation to give him an advertisement, although he was given a summer job in their Chicago packaging department after graduating from Yale. But he was lucky enough to be commissioned for a *Fortune* cover by pure chance: he was in New York showing the art director his portfolio one Friday afternoon when the news came through that the Russian Sputnik had just been launched. *Fortune* quickly had to change the cover and he was asked to produce a design by first thing Monday morning. Still a student, it was the first important step in his professional career.

He left Chicago for Los Angeles, travelling across country by Greyhound bus. Once he got there he called up Saul Bass from a phone box to make an appointment to show his work. Bass gave him some freelance work, and with his earnings he went on to Mexico. He then returned to New York where Paul Rand helped with freelance work, and he was taken on as a temporary assistant by Leo Lionni who was designing the US Pavilion for the Brussels World Fair. Eventually, after knocking on a lot of doors, he got full-time employment in the design department of *Fortune* magazine.

His original plan had not been to work in America, however, but to head south and set up a studio in Venezuela. So, after a year in New York, he left for Caracas. Within four days he had realized it was the wrong move and his decision to leave was encouraged by the outbreak of a local revolution. He escaped to the coast just in time to get on the last boat out, which happened to be bound for Genoa. On arriving in Italy he got a job in the design studio of Pirelli in Milan.

When Fletcher finally returned to London in 1959, it was as a different man: 'I'd grown up and gained a lot of experience.' Many of the influences he encountered in America have shaped subsequent phases of his career, before, during and after Pentagram. Through his *Fortune* connections, Fletcher acquired a three-day-a-week job as a design consultant to *Time and Life* in Europe and taught one day a week at the Central School where Colin Forbes was then the young head of the graphic design department.

Cover. *Graphis* magazine 1960

Poster. Pirelli 1961

Poster. Pirelli 1962

In 1962 Fletcher and Forbes teamed up with an American, Bob Gill, to form Fletcher Forbes Gill – an archetype of the modern graphic design consultancy. According to design historian Christopher Frayling, this group did for graphics in the 1960s what Mary Quant did for clothes. 'We didn't have any work for the first month,' recalls Fletcher. 'We'd go out and sit in a greasy spoon cafe and share one Penguin book jacket between us.' When commissions did begin to arrive, much of it was freelance work from Pirelli, who proved a durable client. A witty Pirelli poster on the side of buses, where the bodies of passengers were drawn below the windows in which their heads appeared, has become one of the graphic icons of the era.

Although graphic design was still largely subsumed within the advertising world, Fletcher Forbes Gill made its mark with irreverent, intelligent and, above all, witty work. But as design in Britain developed in the early 1960s, so the partners began to look at the broader possibilities beyond the boundaries of the graphic disciplines. They had worked with an architect, Theo Crosby, on the graphics for an exhibition at the Milan Triennale. When commissioned to design a new identity for Shell (1964) they proposed that their petrol stations, instead of being buildings, should be constructed out of the letters SHELL. They needed practical advice and so Crosby joined the group: initially 'to make the letters stand up properly,' recalls Fletcher, 'but really to bring his intelligence, charm, skill and experience into the mix.' However, Gill, a designer of occasional genius, never adjusted to the growing multi-disciplinary focus of the work. When Theo Crosby once told him that his designs for a town centre would be built in eight years' time, Gill allegedly replied: 'That's a long time to wait for a proof.' And left. The year was 1965.

At the end of the 1960s a commission to design the pumps and equipment for a new generation of BP self-service petrol stations confirmed the need to extend their abilities even further. By the early 1970s, Fletcher, Forbes, Crosby and Kurlansky, who at that time was their senior designer, were in the frame, and together with product designer Kenneth Grange they decided to form a new group. Simply stringing their surnames together was unwieldy. A new name was needed. The process took nearly a year. There were fierce arguments. The names they liked were already registered. Eventually Alan Fletcher found the name Pentagram in a book on witchcraft: it meant five-pointed star. 'Nobody liked it much but we finally settled on it anyway,' he says . 'Six months later, a designer came up to me during the Warsaw Biennale and said it was a terrible name, we should have called ourselves Pentecost. "Why?" I asked. "Because you charge five times more than anyone else," he replied.'

Poster. PanAm 1972

Rebus. Pentagram 1984

Cover. *Domus* magazine 1994

Pentagram has been one of the most powerful international influences in design since the war. Alan Fletcher was a partner for twenty years from its formation in 1972 to his departure in 1992. Although many of the projects in this book were completed at Pentagram – and he happily acknowledges that often they owe their concept, style and solution to the special ethos of the practice and the interaction between the partners – Pentagram as a creative phenomenon has been well covered elsewhere, not least in the books which the group itself has published. *Beware Wet Paint* takes as its focus the work of Alan Fletcher as an individual.

At Pentagram, he was 'a split personality', veering from the large international corporate identity projects which the practice inevitably attracted, to the more personal and uncommercial projects. These two worlds co-existed for twenty years. Many were shocked at the idea of Pentagram without a man who perhaps epitomized its maverick spirit more than anyone else – but at the same time they were not really surprised. After all, he always appeared to be the most unpredictable and individualistic of a very powerful group of personalities. There was no rift, simply a recognition that he needed to change. 'I found myself taking on jobs I would have preferred to avoid. So I thought I'd start over again but confine myself to the work I like, without the pressures of collective responsibility.'

Today Pentagram has partners in London, New York, Austin and San Francisco. But Alan Fletcher is not among them. They remain his friends but he works on his own in a studio adjoining his home in London, and his career has taken on its own momentum. It is tempting to interpret his decision to go solo in the autumn of 1992 as reflecting his need to concentrate on his own creative obsessions: for some time now he has been establishing a new body of work based on words and sayings. The *Beware Wet Paint* cover design of this book is an example. Around the time he resigned, he wrote that 'painters are concerned with solving their own problems, while designers are concerned with solving other people's problems'. He is a master of both.

Although many of the designs featured in this book are new, it is difficult to distinguish them from those produced in the 1960s, or the 1990s. There is a timelessness to so much of what he produces. His solutions tend not to date. The images retain their vigour, integrity and resonance.

Acknowledgements

This book includes work produced over some thirty-five years. In most cases the projects involved the collaboration and skills of others, as well as the creative input, influence, advice and criticism of my partners, design colleagues, clients, family and friends. They all invariably made me think twice. I acknowledge their encouragement and abrasion. I thank Jeremy Myerson, David Gibbs and Rick Poynor for their patience.

Alan Fletcher

Alan Fletcher's graphic games allow us to play too.
In 1972, he was asked to contribute the April page
to a calendar for a typesetting company. His solution:
1,972 dots which, when you join them all up, spell out
the month, days and dates. What looks like a page of
dandruff disguises a do-it-yourself design. To complete
this book, you could foolishly try to do it yourself.

APRIL 1972

DAY

Phaidon Press Ltd
Regent's Wharf
All Saints Street
London N1 9PA

First published 1996
© 1996 Phaidon Press Ltd

Design by Alan Fletcher
Technics by Mark Facer
Co-ordination and research
by Sarah Copplestone
and Raffaella Fletcher

ISBN 0 7148 3354 1

A CIP catalogue of this
book is available from
the British Library

Printed in Hong Kong